T0316506

Recognition

The idea that we are mutually dependent on the recognition of our peers is at least as old as modernity. Across Europe, this idea has been understood in different ways from the very beginning, according to each country's different cultural and political conditions. This stimulating study explores the complex history and multiple associations of the idea of "Recognition" in Britain, France and Germany. Demonstrating the role of "recognition" in the production of important political ideas, Axel Honneth explores how our dependence on the recognition of others is sometimes viewed as the source of all modern, egalitarian morality, sometimes as a means for fostering socially beneficial behavior, and sometimes as a threat to "true" individuality. By exploring this fundamental concept in our modern political and social self-understanding, Honneth thus offers an alternative view of the philosophical discourse of modernity.

AXEL HONNETH is the Jack C. Weinstein Professor of the Humanities in the Philosophy Department at Columbia University. He was previously Director of the Institute for Social Research in Frankfurt, between 2001 and 2018, founded by Max Horkheimer and Theodor W. Adorno. He is the author of works in German and English, including *The Struggle for Recognition* (1994) and *Freedom's Right: The Social Foundations of Democratic Life* (2014).

THE SEELEY LECTURES

The John Robert Seeley Lectures have been established by the University of Cambridge as a biennial lecture series in social and political studies, sponsored jointly by the Faculty of History and Cambridge University Press. The Seeley Lectures provide a unique forum for distinguished scholars of international reputation to address, in an accessible manner, topics of broad interest in social and political studies. Subsequent to their public delivery in Cambridge, the University Press publishes suitably modified versions of each set of lectures. Professor James Tully delivered the inaugural series of Seeley Lectures in 1994 on the theme of *Constitutionalism in an Age of Diversity*.

The Seeley Lectures include

Strange Multiplicity: Constitutionalism in an Age of Diversity
JAMES TULLY
ISBN 978 0 521 47694 2 (paperback)
Published 1995

The Dignity of Legislation
JEREMY WALDRON
ISBN 978 0 521 65092 2 (hardback) 978 0 521 65883 6 (paperback)
Published 1999

Women and Human Development: The Capabilities Approach
MARTHA C. NUSSBAUM
ISBN 978 0 521 66086 0 (hardback) 978 0 521 00385 8 (paperback)
Published 2000

Value, Respect, and Attachment
JOSEPH RAZ
ISBN 978 0 521 80180 5 (hardback) 978 0 521 00022 2 (paperback)
Published 2001

The Rights of Others: Aliens, Residents, and Citizens
SEYLA BENHABIB
ISBN 978 0 521 83134 5 (hardback) 978 0 521 53860 2 (paperback)
Published 2004

Laws of Fear: Beyond the Precautionary Principle
CASS R. SUNSTEIN
ISBN 978 0 521 84823 7 (hardback) 978 0 521 61512 9 (paperback)
Published 2005

Counter-Democracy: Politics in an Age of Distrust
PIERRE ROSANVALLON
ISBN 978 0 521 86622 2 (hardback) 978 0 521 71383 2 (paperback)
Published 2008

On the People's Terms: A Republican Theory and Model of Democracy
PHILIP PETTIT
ISBN 978 1 107 00511 2 (hardback) 978 0 521 18212 6 (paperback)
Published 2012

The Politics of the Human
ANNE PHILLIPS
ISBN 978 1 107 093973 (hardback) 978 1 107 475830 (paperback)
Published 2015

The Sleeping Sovereign: The Invention of Modern Democracy
RICHARD TUCK
ISBN 978 1 107 130142 (hardback) 978 1 107 570580 (paperback)
Published 2015

Recognition: A Chapter in the History of European Ideas
AXEL HONNETH
ISBN 978 1 108 836869 (hardback) 978 1 108 819305 (paperback)
Published 2021

RECOGNITION

A Chapter in the History of European Ideas

AXEL HONNETH
Columbia University, New York

Translated by
JOSEPH GANAHL

CAMBRIDGE
UNIVERSITY PRESS

CAMBRIDGE
UNIVERSITY PRESS

University Printing House, Cambridge CB2 8BS, United Kingdom

One Liberty Plaza, 20th Floor, New York, NY 10006, USA

477 Williamstown Road, Port Melbourne, VIC 3207, Australia

314-321, 3rd Floor, Plot 3, Splendor Forum, Jasola District Centre, New Delhi - 110025, India

79 Anson Road, #06-04/06, Singapore 079906

Cambridge University Press is part of the University of Cambridge.

It furthers the University's mission by disseminating knowledge in the pursuit of education, learning and research at the highest international levels of excellence.

www.cambridge.org
Information on this title: www.cambridge.org/9781108819305
DOI: 10.1017/9781108872775

First published 2021

A catalogue record for this publication is available from the British Library

ISBN 978-1-108-83686-9 Hardback
ISBN 978-1-108-81930-5 Paperback

Gratefully dedicated to Jürgen Habermas

CONTENTS

This study began with an invitation by the Cambridge Centre
of Political Thought to hold the biennial John Robert Seeley
Lectures at the University of Cambridge in May 2017.
Admittedly I was rather intimidated by the enormous reputation of this institution as a melting pot of intellectual history,
so I chose the path of caution and decided to focus on
a subject that clearly belongs to the history of ideas, and yet
still is a subject about which I could claim a certain measure of
theoretical authority. I planned to venture into the arena of
the history of political thought, while still keeping to familiar
philosophical ground. Thus arose the idea for my Seeley
Lectures and for this book. Just as the so-called Cambridge
School and the German "history of concepts"
[Begriffsgeschichte] have managed to reconstruct the complicated and conflict-laden history of several key concepts in our
political self-understanding, thereby providing insight into
the historical origin of major democratic ideas, I will use the
modest tools at my disposal to do the same for another idea
that has become relatively significant: recognition. In the
following five chapters I will attempt to uncover the historical
roots of an idea we now take for granted: the idea that relations between subjects are defined by mutual dependence on
esteem or recognition.

The first difficulty posed by this task is that the idea of
recognition has come to be associated with so many different

things in different contexts. Our dependence on others' recognition is sometimes viewed as the source of all modern, egalitarian morality, sometimes as a mere social means for fostering socially beneficial behavior, and sometimes it is viewed as a threat to "true" individuality, the root of a fatal self-deception about "authentic" personality. As we will see, some of these differences are linked to semantic particularities of the concept of recognition in various linguistic cultures; for instance, unlike "reconnaissance" in French and "recognition" in English, the German term "Anerkennung" does not connote *re*-cognition in the sense of esteeming each other *again*.[1] Other differences derive from chains of association that have seeped into the local meanings of these terms over the course of their use in various specific cultures. One crucial distinction in the theoretical usage of the concept is whether recognition refers to a person's social reputation or to something more profound and independent of how that person is viewed by the public. An equally important distinction is whether recognition is considered a moral act, a manner of conveying respect or an epistemic occurrence, a result of our having recognized an independent entity. Both semantic distinctions and diverse chains of association in local cultural contexts play a crucial role when it comes to reconstructing the modern history of the idea of recognition. Before I take up this task, I would first like to express my gratitude to those whose invitation motivated me to consider undertaking such

---

[1] See Paul Ricoeur, *The Course of Recognition* (Cambridge, MA: Harvard University Press, 2005); Heikki Ikäheimo, *Anerkennung* (Berlin and Boston: de Gruyter, 2014).

an investigation in the first place. Above all I am grateful to John Robertson, who as Director of the Cambridge Centre for Political Thought invited me to hold the Seeley Lectures in Cambridge in 2017. Not only did his generous hospitality allow me to enjoy my stay thoroughly at the university, but his insightful questions, rooted in a profound knowledge of the European Enlightenment, also contributed significantly to refining my view of the intellectual development of the idea of recognition. I also owe my gratitude to John Dunn, Christopher Meckstroth and Michael Sonenscher, whose comments and objections prevented me from drawing overly hasty and imprudent conclusions. I would also like to thank Michael Nance, who spent two semesters as a Humboldt Fellow in the Institute of Philosophy at the Goethe University in Frankfurt, for his vital impulses and remarks on the notion of recognition in German Idealism, the subject of the fourth chapter of my study. The most crucial motivation to turn my lectures into a book came from Elizabeth Friend-Smith of Cambridge University Press and Eva Gilmer of Suhrkamp Verlag; their gentle pressure and friendly reminders ensured a punctual delivery of the manuscript. I would also like to thank Eva Gilmer for reviewing my manuscript, a custom of which I have almost grown fond, with such great care and precision. Finally, I thank the translator of this edition, Joseph Ganahl, for his care and energy in providing a faithful translation of my work.

1

Methodological Remarks on the History of Ideas vs. the History of Concepts

As I mentioned in the preface, it is important for our democratic culture that we recall the historical origins and developments of the ideas and concepts that continue to define our political and cultural life today. Only on the basis of such historical reflection can we recognize how we have become who we are and which normative claims are entailed by our shared self-understanding. The concept of "recognition" merits such historical reflection as well; after all, over the last few decades, it has become a crucial element of our political and cultural self-understanding, as is illustrated by demands that we respect each other as equally entitled members of a cooperative community,[1] that we unconditionally recognize the particularity of others[2] or respect cultural minorities in the context of a "politics of recognition".[3] By reconstructing the modern history of the idea of recognition, I hope to sort out the many various meanings of recognition and thus contribute to clarifying our current political and cultural

---

[1] John Rawls, *Justice as Fairness: A Restatement* (Cambridge, MA: Harvard University Press, 2001), esp. ch. 2.

[2] Judith Butler, *Giving an Account of Oneself* (New York: Fordham University Press, 2005).

[3] Charles Taylor, *Multiculturalism and the Politics of Recognition* (Princeton: Princeton University Press, 1992).

self-understanding. Before I can directly turn to this task, however, I need to say a few words about both my approach and my aims, for the attempt to uncover the origins of our current understanding of recognition is faced with demands and expectations of varying complexity and sophistication.

For various reasons, there are two narrow limits on my historical approach to the concept of recognition: first, it would be highly misleading to suggest that my attempt to uncover the historical origins of recognition is only concerned with this single term. Unlike other concepts of similar importance, i.e. the "state", "freedom" or "sovereignty", there has not always been a single, identical term to denote what we mean by "recognition". On the contrary, a great number of terms have been employed in modernity to express the fact that we are related to each other by means of various forms of recognition: Rousseau drew on the work of the French moralists in using the term "amour propre", Adam Smith spoke of an internal "external observer", and it was not until Fichte and Hegel came along that the now familiar term "recognition" came into use. The origin and development of the contemporary idea of recognition thus cannot be revealed merely by examining the historical use of just this one term. We would thereby lose sight of too many relevant currents, too many significant sources and ideas. Therefore, I will not undertake a history of the concept in this narrow sense; rather I will trace the development of a constitutive thought by studying the various meanings that have become attached to it by virtue of having either corrected it or added to it. This means I will have to begin with the difficult question of whether we can find something like a "big bang" for the concept of recognition.

Of course, there are many ways to undertake a "conceptual history" of "recognition". Thinkers such as Robin G. Collingwood, Quentin Skinner, Michel Foucault and Reinhart Koselleck, to name just a few, have developed very different conceptions of what it would mean to reconstruct the origins and history of specific ideas. However, my investigation into the genesis of our current idea of "recognition" does not attempt to live up to the demands of the history of ideas as a scientific discipline. Nor will I make an effort to untangle the complicated historical relationship of causality among different versions of one and the same vague idea. To undertake such a historical study in the true sense of the term would require, paraphrasing Dummett, providing evidence that certain thinkers were in fact influenced by certain other thinkers. In order to do so, "dates of publication must be scrutinised, diaries and personal correspondence studied, even library catalogues examined to discover what specific individuals read or might have read."[4] I feel incapable of undertaking such a task given the means that my own academic education has put at my disposal. I have never learned how to undertake bibliographical research, nor am I accustomed to tracing intellectual influences back to their historical source. Therefore, we will have to content ourselves with a "conceptual history" whose standards are far lower than those set by the discipline which normally goes by this name. The following study will instead focus on how a certain thought, i.e. recognition, followed different developmental paths, taking on ever new and revealing meanings by virtue of the fact that this

---

[4] Michael Dummett, *Origins of Analytical Philosophy* (Cambridge, MA: Harvard University Press, 1993), p. 2.

idea was "in the air", so to say. Whether the various descendants of this single idea will ultimately coincide and furnish us with a unified concept or instead remain mere fragments is a question I will deal with at the end of my historical reconstruction. At any rate I intend to provide a history of the argumentative development of an idea, not to present the causal sequence of how one author influenced the next. Do not expect any new discoveries of intellectual constellations or influences; at most you will receive a different perspective on already familiar material.

There is one point, however, at which I hope to manage to go beyond the already familiar results of the history of modern ideas: I will place special emphasis on the question of whether the particular sociocultural conditions in a given country have lent a specific coloring to the idea of recognition. Because the notion that we are always already involved in relations of recognition has taken on such a variety of meanings in modern thought, I will operate on the hypothesis that these differences are linked to the national particularities of the cultures in which the term is employed. By making such an admittedly risky presupposition, obviously I am forced to adopt a particular approach: I will not deal with individual authors in a way that focuses on the individuality of their respective works; rather I must treat several authors of the same nationality as typical representatives of a larger group sharing certain theoretical beliefs and ethical valuations. I will thus have to treat individual works as instances of a common culture, so it should be no surprise that in the following chapters I will focus on the national particularities of the usage of the term "recognition".

Of course, I am aware that I thereby run the risk of following a tradition that speaks, intentionally or unintentionally, of the "spirit" or "soul" of a nation. We should be wary – especially those of us from Germany – of naively reviving notions of "national" dispositions that can be ascribed to an entire people. Therefore, I will in no way refer to collective "attitudes", national mentalities and the like; by speaking of national particularities concerning the idea of recognition, I mean to say that the sociocultural conditions of a certain country may have influenced a number of thinkers within that country to make similar associations with the idea of recognition. What I have in mind is essentially that which justifies our asking whether certain motives, themes or styles of thought prevailing in the philosophical tradition of a given country derive from the latter's distinct institutional or social conditions.[5] I will operate on the assumption that the national particularities emerging in the course of a nation's historical development are what cause the idea of recognition to take on a specific tone or coloring depending on the country under discussion.

I am certainly not the first to have noticed that the idea that we are mutually dependent on others' recognition has a negative connotation in French thought. Beginning with Rousseau at the latest and extending into the work of Sartre or Lacan, our dependence on the social esteem or affirmation of others represents the danger of losing ourselves in our own, entirely unique individuality. Regardless of how this thought is further elucidated and justified in detail, its continual reappearance in the works of a number of French authors allows us to presume that this negative connotation is not a coincidence, but

---

[5] See my essay "Zwischen den Generationen", *Merkur*, no. 610 (2000), pp. 147–52.

that certain national particularities must have played a certain role in the matter. This in turn raises the question of which particularities in the social and cultural history of France might have caused the idea of recognition to take on such a negative connotation. And once we have chosen to go down this path, it will make sense to search in other countries for similar links between the sociocultural conditions in a given country and the prevailing understanding of recognition. From here it is but a small step to the hypothesis that differences in the experiential horizons of various philosophical cultures contribute to the fact that a single idea has come to have such disparate meanings over the course of the last three centuries.

Yet, this still does not explain why I have chosen to focus on France, Great Britain and Germany. This is due, first of all, to pragmatic reasons, as the shifts in political thought in these countries over the course of modernity are particularly well-researched. The changes in the political and cultural self-understanding of these countries over the last three or four centuries are much more familiar to us than the contemporary and equally relevant shifts in other countries on the European continent. Perhaps the fact that these three countries occupy such a central position in the history of ideas is also due to the fact that these nations' authors are regarded almost exclusively as having produced the "classics" of political thought. With very few exceptions, e.g. Baruch de Spinoza and perhaps Francisco Suárez, the political thinkers whose works fill our textbooks today originate from the French-, English- or German-speaking parts of Europe. It is all but inevitable that we ask whether this obvious dominance merely reflects the theoretical imperialism of three powerful nations or whether it is due instead to the substance of their work.

Merely by raising this question, it becomes obvious that pragmatic reasons cannot suffice to justify my focusing on these three particular countries. If I left it at that, I would inevitably be suspected of merely regurgitating the philosophical perspective of the dominant European powers. In order to dispel such concerns, I cannot merely refer to the state of current research or the customs of the discipline. Perhaps it will help to cite a consideration I first encountered in an essay by Reinhart Koselleck and have encountered in a number of other studies. Koselleck believes that the historical developments in modern France, Great Britain and Germany since the seventeenth century reflect three developmental patterns in civil or bourgeois society over the course of modernity. Not only do the bourgeoisies in these three countries differ in terms of how they understand their role and historical position, a fact revealed by the different meanings of "citoyen", "Bürger" and the "middle classes", but these semantic differences also indicate the fundamental alternatives with respect to how the new social order could develop.[6] A similar argument is made by Jerrold Seigel in his comprehensive study *Modernity and Bourgeois Life*, in which he addresses the differences in the self-understanding of the bourgeoisie and investigates the paths of modernization taken by France, Great Britain and Germany.

---

[6] Reinhart Koselleck, "Drei bürgerliche Welten? Zur vergleichenden Semantik der bürgerlichen Gesellschaft in Deutschland, England und Frankreich", in *Begriffsgeschichten: Studien zur Semantik und Pragmatik der politischen und sozialen Sprache* (Frankfurt: Suhrkamp, 2006).

Like Koselleck, he operates on the premise that these do not merely represent three random examples, but rather the paradigmatic patterns of development of bourgeois society in modern Europe.[7] If we pursue this basic line of thought further, we will come upon an argument that might allow me to justify limiting my project to the history of ideas in a mere three countries. If it is true, as Koselleck and Seigel seem to suggest, that the intellectual and societal changes in France, Great Britain and Germany over the course of the last three centuries provide the structure and the model for developments in the rest of Europe as well, then my focus on these three countries would be based on more than merely random or pragmatic considerations. Instead, the semantic coloring and accents that the idea of "recognition" has taken on in these three countries would reflect the only variations of which the European horizon of consciousness has proven capable. Because this might sound a bit presumptuous, I would like to formulate the matter a bit more cautiously. If it is true that the three types of development undergone by bourgeois society and paradigmatic for all of Europe can be found in the self-understanding of the bourgeoisies in France, Great Britain and Germany, then a historical analysis of the changes and colorings of the idea of recognition in these countries would largely exhaust the meanings this term can have.

This idea is the basis for my hope that the following inquiry into the origins and developments of the idea of

---

[7] Jerrold Seigel, *Modernity and Bourgeois Life: Society, Politics, and Culture in England, France, and Germany since 1750* (Cambridge: Cambridge University Press, 2012).

recognition in modern Europe will not merely reflect one particular point of view. Although interesting and illuminating meanings of the idea of recognition might also be found in other linguistic regions of Europe, they have not managed to establish themselves as enduring connotations of the term. For reasons that will soon become clear, I will begin my analysis in the francophone realm. It is here that the notion that we always already relate to each other by means of mutual recognition first took root, leading to a very specific, nationally colored conception of intersubjectivity.

2

From Rousseau to Sartre
Recognition and Loss of Self

For some time now there has been a wide-ranging and complex discussion about which modern thinker should be credited with having launched the idea of recognition. Thirty years ago, it was largely agreed that Fichte or Hegel came up with the idea, at the same time paving the way for the entire theory of recognition. In the meantime things have changed significantly, with a virtual flood of proposals pushing the birth date of the idea of recognition ever further into the past, tracing its origins back to much earlier thinkers.[1] Istvan Hont has made the boldest claim in this debate over philosophical authorship and intellectual ancestry, arguing in *Politics in Commercial Society* that

---

[1] Istvan Hont names Hobbes, Rousseau and Smith in particular: *Politics in Commercial Society: Jean-Jacques Rousseau and Adam Smith* (Cambridge, MA: Harvard University Press, 2015) (Hobbes); Frederick Neuhouser, *Rousseau's Theodicy of Self-Love: Evil, Rationality and the Drive for Recognition* (Oxford: Oxford University Press, 2008) (Rousseau); Stephen Darwall, "Equal Dignity in Adam Smith", *Adam Smith Review* 1 (2004), pp. 129–34 (Smith). See also the interesting collection Francesco Toto, Théophile Penigaud de Mourgues and Emmanuel Renault, eds, *Le reconnaissance avant la reconnaissance: Archéologie d'une problematique moderne* (Lyon: ENS, 2017).

Thomas Hobbes was in fact the first to emphasize the paramount importance of recognition for human coexistence. He considers Hobbes' work to be so new and groundbreaking because of his insight that humans are motivated to associate and coexist with others in social units less because of "physical" needs than because of the "psychological" desire for honor and distinction.[2] Certainly Hont is right to point out that the author of Leviathan consistently emphasized the degree to which individual subjects desire to be considered honorable and exceptional by their fellow humans. More than any of his predecessors', Hobbes' political anthropology takes account of the fact that pride, the craving for recognition and the desire to stand out of the crowd are what motivate humans to make contact with each other.[3] But to declare Hobbes the progenitor of the modern theory of recognition would mean proving that such "psychological" human desires are found at the core of his political philosophy. As far as I can tell, this is not the case. His notion of the social contract is based on his claim that individuals in the state of nature are so deeply concerned for their physical safety that they prefer to be subjected to a ruler who can guarantee their safety. The monarch enthroned on the basis of such strategic calculations by isolated subjects in turn is charged primarily with ensuring political stability rather than with satisfying the

[2] Hont, *Politics in Commercial Society*, pp. 10ff.
[3] See for instance Thomas Hobbes, "On the State of Man Without Civil Society", in *On the Citizen*, ed. Richard Tuck and Michael Silverthorne (Cambridge: Cambridge University Press, 1998), pp. 21–31; Hobbes, *Leviathan* (Cambridge: Cambridge University Press, 1993), ch. 10.

desire for social recognition.[4] These two decisive steps taken by Hobbes in *Leviathan* make it improbable that he should be credited as the first thinker to assert the full weight of our need for social recognition. It is much more convincing to take note of the significant gap between Hobbes' psychological-anthropological insights and his political theory, in which there is little trace of the former.

Therefore, I want to go down a different path and attempt to find the origins of the theory of recognition in the work of Rousseau and his predecessors in seventeenth-century French moralism – though I should note that the notion that we humans are constitutively dependent upon recognition was "in the air" in many European countries at the time. As the first, still hesitant thrusts of modernization began to undermine the previous social order, traditional social bonds and class affiliations also began to dissolve across Europe. The less the prevailing social structure could be regarded as being determined and desired by God, the more individuals were forced to question the reasons for the position they occupied or desired to occupy within society. To say it more pointedly, the gradual transition from the feudal order to modern class society is what pushed the question of social recognition to the forefront throughout Europe. Once a person's social position and the attendant demands on behavior were no longer settled, the fact that we relate to each other by means of various forms of recognition became a major topic of philosophy and literature. Over the course of the seventeenth and eighteenth

[4] Hobbes, *Leviathan*, ch. 30

centuries in France, this problem not only took on a particular urgency, but also a very specific tone. A kind of "negative anthropology"[5] quickly emerged in the wake of the question concerning the foundation of individuals' position within society, ascribing to such uncertain subjects the desire to be regarded as "better" or "more" than they truly are. Recognition therefore had to be viewed as a very risky enterprise in which it could never be clear whether it really captured the "true" essence of others. My claim is that up to the present day, this pervasive, implicit suspicion would come to accompany the discourse on recognition in France like a malignant shadow.

The concept that would become the bearer of this new social idea in France was that of "amour propre". Even before Rousseau could systematically develop this concept as the foundation of his own theory of recognition, French moralists employed it as a means of questioning traditional conceptions of human nature. François, duc de La Rochefoucauld led the way in pointing out his contemporaries' deep-seated inclination for publicly casting themselves in a flattering light and warned of misjudging one's own individual behavior and traits. To this end he offered a secular reinterpretation of an antimony raised by Augustine. Whereas Christian theologians saw "superbia" or vanity as being opposed to the virtue of a godly, sociable form of self-love, this French moralist retained only the one pole of this dualism, complacency, which he no longer regarded as

---

[5] The proposal that we regard the anthropology of French moralists as "negative" stems from Karlheinz Stierle, *Montaigne und die Moralisten* (Paderborn: Wilhelm Fink, 2016).

a violation of ethics but as a natural human passion.[6] To describe this natural drive he used the term "amour propre" – an expression which stems from the young Montaigne,[7] is difficult to translate and is best captured, if at all, by terms such as "vanity" or a "craving for recognition". In any case, the disposition indicated by this term is the point around which his famous *Maxims* revolve. Here we see the new semantics at work in that whenever individuals behave with virtue, stature or moral excellence, they are suspected of merely feigning characteristics they do not truly possess. What truly motivates humans and moves them to feign socially esteemed characteristics is in La Rochefoucauld's eyes merely their "amour propre", their "impetuous desires" (*désirs impétueux*) to be regarded as exemplary and excellent.[8]

What concerns La Rochefoucauld about this natural human passion enough to dedicate over 500 aphorisms to it is not only the idea that our necessary uncertainty about the true character of our partners in interaction plunges us into epistemic uncertainty. Just as alarming for him is the possibility that the deception entailed by "amour propre" could cause individuals to forget their true nature. In his famous 119th maxim he states the matter briefly: "We are so used to

---

[6] Paul Geyer, *Die Entdeckung des modernen Subjekts: Anthropologie von Descartes bis Rousseau* (Tübingen: Königshausen & Neumann, 1997), pp. 64–8.

[7] Hans-Jürgen Fuchs, *Entfremdung und Narzißmus: Semantische Untersuchungen zur Geschichte der "Selbstbezogenheit" als Vorgeschichte von französisch "amour propre"* (Stuttgart: Metzler, 1977).

[8] François, duc de La Rochefoucauld, *Maxims* (Oxford: Penguin Classics, 1959). On "impetuous" or "vehement" desires, see Maxim 563.TRANS?

disguising ourselves from others that we end by disguising ourselves from ourselves."[9] For La Rochefoucauld, therefore, "amour propre" is a basic human drive that affects others and ourselves, i.e. our relation-to-self. When facing others, we are driven to feign socially esteemed characteristics that we do not truly possess; and when facing ourselves, we grow so accustomed to deception that we fail to recognize our own true character. La Rochefoucauld thus regarded both temptations – to deceive others and ourselves – as alarming and even dangerous, as they threatened to rob us of any chance of self-determination, of our capacity for autonomy.[10]

Now, La Rochefoucauld was not enough of a philosopher or academic to follow up on these clever insights with more than a few biting *bon mots*; he lacked both the historical awareness and the conceptual precision needed to turn the understanding of the workings of "amour propre" into the core of a comprehensive understanding of human intersubjectivity. On the other hand, he never intended to contribute to our knowledge of the dynamics and conflicted nature of social interactions; his witty remarks, intended for use in the convivial atmosphere of the salon, did not aim to develop a theory or expand our scientific knowledge, but to expose the vanity of his contemporaries. Disappointed at the failure of the Fronde in their struggle against Louis XIV's marginalization of the nobility, a struggle in which La Rochefoucauld stood on the

---

[9] Ibid., Maxim 11.

[10] See Jürgen von Stackelberg, 'Nachwort', in La Rochefoucauld, *Maximes et réflexions morales/Maximen und Reflexionen* (Stuttgart: Reclam, 2012), pp. 265–87, here p. 285f.

front lines, he bore witness to the vain attempts of his former comrades to feign honorable virtues and thus win the favor of the king. The birth of the theory of recognition in French thought was the moment members of the nobility began to suspiciously eye each other's techniques of showing off and currying favor in the royal court.

La Rochefoucauld's work was absolutely decisive for the direction that the theory of recognition would take in France over the course of the following centuries. The concept of "amour propre", which he made fruitful for the study of intersubjective relationships, focused from the very beginning on a dimension of "recognition" that was not necessarily self-evident. As I have shown above, that which later came to be indicated by this term was conceived of from the perspective of a subject driven by the desire to appear excellent or superior to other people. By seeking the "recognition" or, better, the "esteem" of others, the subject constantly desires to appear to possess characteristics it does not truly possess – those which enjoy particular respect in its own respective culture. This natural tendency to make ourselves appear to be "more" than we truly are raises a problem for both the judging public and the judged subject – the epistemic nature of which is already clear in the work of La Rochefoucauld. Both the judging authority that grants recognition and the individual who strives for recognition will necessarily come to question whether the virtues a person displays in fact reflect that person's true characteristics. As a result of this epistemic turn, the act of recognition acquires a meaning which clearly corresponds to the cognitive element of the French term "reconnaissance"; at stake in the recognition or esteem of another person is always also the *cognition* of what is "objectively" the case. However, because La Rochefoucauld never used the term "recognition" in his writings, the semantic ambiguity of the word in French cannot be the reason for his tendency to describe intersubjective evaluation primarily as a problem of cognizing states of affairs. What could have instead played a major role is the fact that La Rochefoucauld gathered the material for his insights into the poisonous effects of "amour propre" from intrigues in the royal court, where individual success was predicated on recognizing whether one's competitors were truly virtuous or merely feigning virtue.

Nowhere else in seventeenth-century Europe was the "representative publicness" of the feudal nobility so strongly concentrated in the royal court as in France, the place where La Rochefoucauld wrote his maxims.[11] Having mostly lost their political power after the failure of the Fronde uprisings, members of the nobility, now aiming to preserve whatever privileges they still retained, gathered around the monarch and those he trusted most in order to gain advantageous influence – be it by intrigue or by displaying excellence and manners. If strategic machinations and maneuvers did not do the trick, then one had to appear as an exemplary individual and display esteemed virtues in order to prove worthy of the approval of the king and his court.[12] If we grasp

---

[11] On the representative publicness of the feudal nobility, see Jürgen Habermas, *The Structural Transformation of the Public Sphere* (Cambridge, MA: MIT Press, 1991), pp. 12ff.

[12] See esp. Norbert Elias, *The Court Society* (Dublin: UCD Press, 2006); see also Fuchs, *Entfremdung und Narzißmus*, pp. 259ff.

La Rochefoucauld's writings as an attempt to separate the wheat from the chaff, to distinguish between mere bluffs and true stature, then it is easy to understand the epistemic tone of his concept of "amour propre". Although he used the term to characterize a general human desire, it was originally intended to raise the possibility that an individual could in fact feign characteristics it does not truly possess. We will see that even today, this epistemic turn in the idea of recognition at a very early stage remains a part of French thought.

As early as Rousseau, who today is often regarded as the progenitor of the modern theory of recognition,[13] the concept of our dependence on others' evaluations sways peculiarly between epistemic and moral contexts. Even apart from the fact that the term "amour propre" plays a major role in Rousseau's writings, it is obvious that the author of *The Social Contract* was influenced by French moralism, in particular by La Rochefoucauld and Montaigne, upon whose sharp-tongued observations he often drew. His reliance on the skeptical anthropology of his predecessors is already made apparent by the fact that he suspects all human behavior that appears excellent or cognitively superior to be in fact mere show. Certainly, the political and sociocultural conditions in France had changed significantly over the hundred years that lie between the writings of the moralists and those of Rousseau. Although the political foundations of the Ancien Régime remained intact, the struggle for the favor of the royal court had come to involve not only the members of the aristocracy, who by this time had been rendered all but powerless, but also the rising bourgeoisie.

---

[13] See Neuhouser, *Rousseau's Theodicy of Self-Love.*

For this newly emergent class, whose wealth had grown rapidly due to the general rise of trade and commerce, the only real way to attain political influence, lucrative positions and financial privileges was to gain the approval of the absolutist monarch. With the rise of the bourgeoisie, however, the cultural means of gaining the attention and the favor of the royal court had also changed. No longer did competitors display their respect for traditional aristocratic customs of decency and virtue; rather the court came to regard the demonstration of a debonair attitude, luxury and fashionable dress as superior forms of showing honor once the modest beginnings of advertisement and mass communication had begun to pave the way for fashion.[14]

During Rousseau's work on what is often considered a kind of "cultural criticism", the competition between the nobility and the bourgeoisie for the favor of the king in Paris and Versailles had begun to take on rather odd forms. In 1755 Rousseau published his *Discourse on Inequality*, in which the poisonous effects of "amour propre" play a central role in explaining the rise of social inequality.[15] In his famous *Letter to D'Alembert*, which followed in 1758, he accuses the theatre of endangering political morals by encouraging role-play on stage, thus teaching the audience how to feign personal qualities one does not truly possess, infecting them with the virus of "mere appearances".[16] The theoretical bond joining these

---

[14] See Seigel, *Modernity and Bourgeois Life*, pp. 85–91.

[15] Jean-Jacques Rousseau, *Discourse on Inequality* (Oxford: Oxford University Press, 1994).

[16] Jean-Jaques Rousseau, "Letter to M. D'Alembert on the Theatre", in *Politics and the Arts* (Glencoe, IL: The Free Press, 1960), pp. 92–138. See also the very illuminating interpretation given by Juliane Rebentisch, *The*

two works and lending them their systematic sharpness is a claim whose conceptual origin is found in the work of La Rochefoucauld, but whose philosophical import extends far beyond the latter's merely sensual and pedagogic intentions. In Rousseau's eyes, the dynamic of "amour propre", the craving for recognition noted by French moralists, is so strengthened by rapid shifts in the standards for granting recognition that it brings forth ever more outlandish forms of brashness and demonstrative social superiority. The theatre provides a forum for such dubious behavior by presenting the art of deception as a model to be followed, potentially seducing the audience into feigning socially valued personality traits. By contrast, the dynamic nature of the craving for recognition leaves its mark on the social structure by inexorably widening the gap between the dominant and lower classes. Rousseau's early contemporary diagnosis therefore offers a much more precise and profound determination of the features of "amour propre"; the latter is regarded as having such a capacity for dynamism and self-reinvention due to the fact that it relies on criteria of social esteem that quickly wear out as a result of widespread imitation. Rousseau arrives at these insights by going a conceptual step beyond his moralist predecessors: He invokes – whether he does so consciously or blindly is immaterial – Augustine's antimony between divinely ordained self-love and mere vanity in order to explore further the true nature of "amour propre". He takes this step in his *Discourse on the Origins and Foundation*

Art of Freedom: On the Dialectics of Democratic Existence (Cambridge: Polity Press, 2016), ch. 5.

of Inequality Among Mankind, and it is here that he provides his reasoning for what we can justifiably call a negative theory of recognition. Although this treatise ostensibly deals with the issue of social inequality, its theoretical core lies in the concept of "amour propre". In his attempt to explain the causes of the rise of artificial hierarchies, i.e. hierarchies not based on physical differences, Rousseau realized that the latter could not be fully explained by natural drives, emotions or passions. These he viewed as essentially consisting in the self-referential drive to survive, the intention to perfect one's survival skills, and lastly, deep-seated feelings of empathy,[17] none of which could fully explain why humans should strive to achieve superiority over their peers. In order to bridge this explanatory gap, Rousseau introduces the passion of "amour propre", viewing it as a historically emergent need to appear especially valuable, superior and thus to stand above others in the social hierarchy. Once he realized that this strange desire, contrary to what the moralists had assumed, originated in culture and by virtue of habit, and thus belonged to humans' second rather than their first nature, Rousseau would seek to explain this desire by comparing it to the primitive, merely self-referential desire for survival. In order to make this distinction, and apparently following the terminology employed by his contemporary Vauvenargues,[18] he employed the conceptual pair "amour de soi" and "amour propre", thus reviving Augustine's dualism in a secular form.

---

[17] Rousseau, *Discourse on Inequality*, p. 167.
[18] Fuchs, *Entfremdung und Narzißmus*, p. 287.

Given the major significance of this conceptual dichotomy in *Discourse on Inequality*, it is astounding that Rousseau dedicates no more than a few lines to it.[19] Essentially everything he has to say about this dichotomy can be found in a single footnote, in remark XV. And yet this remark is so compact and rich in substance that it illuminates why these two desires or needs should entail two entirely different kinds of human self-relation.[20] Rousseau derives the distinction between "amour de soi" and "amour propre" from their distinct criteria for judging the appropriateness of our actions. In the case of "amour de soi", we follow the natural need to judge our actions according to criteria drawn entirely from our own judgment and our instinct for what is good and right for us. By contrast, when we follow our "amour propre", a need we acquire through socialization and cultural habituation, we make our actions dependent upon the judgment of others, as we desire to receive their approval or recognition for our actions. Rousseau formulates this contrast most clearly when he introduces the "inner observer" and states that subjects seeking to satisfy their "amour de soi" are their own sole spectators, whereas in the case of "amour propre" they regard their peers as "judges" of their actions.[21] Rousseau almost certainly owes this play on words to his reading of the writings on morality of David Hume,[22] to whom Rousseau maintains

---

[19] Rousseau, *Discourse on Inequality*, pp. 45, 47, 95.

[20] Ibid., Note O, pp. 115–16. [21] Ibid., p. 116.

[22] On the relationship between Rousseau and David Hume, see the fascinating account by Robert Zaretzky and John T. Scott, *The Philosophers' Quarrel: Rousseau, Hume, and the Limits of Human Understanding* (New Haven: Yale University Press, 2009); see also

a bizarre relation somewhere between affection and rejection. If Hume is indeed the father to this thought, then this would also illustrate how little we should take it for granted that others' judgment of the appropriateness of our own actions is as questionable or even problematic as Rousseau suggests when he speaks of "amour propre". Hume and Adam Smith were both convinced that when our actions are subject to the judgment of our peers, they will turn out far superior to those that are merely self-referential in terms of caution, maturity and appropriateness.[23] Rousseau, therefore, must have his own reasons for assuming that judging our own behavior from the perspective of the internalized judgment of other subjects only contributes to our harmful craving for recognition and social distinction. The Genevan philosopher obviously defines this internalized observer quite differently from his Scottish contemporaries if he assumes that it is harmful to both individuals and society. For Rousseau, external "judges" of our actions do not ensure the quality of our judgments or foster cognitive and moral decentering, but rather constantly stoke our desire to be superior to our peers.

Dennis C. Rasmussen, *The Infidel and The Professor: David Hume, Adam Smith, and the Friendship that Shaped Modern Thought* (Princeton: Princeton University Press, 2017), ch. 7.

[23] It is very much worth reading Hina Nazar's account "The Eyes of Others: Rousseau and Adam Smith on Judgment and Autonomy", in Thomas Pfau and Vivasvan Soni, eds, *Judgment and Action: Fragments Toward a History* (Chicago: Northwestern University Press, 2017), pp. 113–41. On the relationship between Rousseau and Adam Smith, see also Dennis C. Rasmussen, *The Problems and Promise of Commercial Society: Adam Smith's Response to Rousseau* (University Park: Pennsylvania State University Press, 2018), esp. pp. 59–71.

This remarkable discrepancy derives from the fact that Rousseau assumes that subjects who are aware of the observation and judgment of their peers follow a desire which plays a marginal role at most in the writings of Smith and Hume. For Rousseau, as soon as an individual feels the judging gaze of its peers, it will strive to appear better or more valuable than others. We could make it easy on ourselves and merely speculate whether this notable turn in the image of the subject is associated with the cultural differences in public life in contemporary France and Great Britain. In Rousseau's Paris, there is the vain struggle for the favor of the pompous king; in Hume and Smith's Edinburgh, there are the peaceful, highly moderate workings of a kingdom governed fairly well by parliament. But such an explanation would not only be historically superficial, but would also fail to do justice to Rousseau's own argument. One likely reason for his belief that the mere adoption of the perspective of others gives rise to a craving for recognition is that contrary to Hume and Smith, Rousseau believes that not only individual behavior, but also personal merits are thereby judged. According to Rousseau, individuals feel the need to prove to their internalized judge that they are capable of doing and achieving something, but not that they obey shared rules and norms. Although this distinction might appear insignificant, it is in fact quite crucial, for it is only in the case of achievement or capacity that the idea of more or less, better or worse comes into play at all. If the point was only to prove that we can conform to prevailing norms, it would suffice to be as good or competent as others; but if we must demonstrate a special ability or achievement, then we assume a criterion for comparison. Whether I truly have achieved something, whether my actions in fact reveal a special ability, can only be judged by resorting to a criterion of success. This appears to be precisely the scenario that Rousseau has in mind when he remarks that the perspective of society and the craving for recognition share a common origin. As soon as individuals act according to the anticipated judgment of their peers, they will feel compelled to prove their superiority, as there is no other way to prove their excellence to their own internalized judge. The kind of social recognition sought in the case of "amour propre" is, as Frederick Neuhouser has shown, doubly relational:[24] On the one hand, individuals strive to be esteemed *in comparison* to others; on the other hand, what they desire to be esteemed for is a capacity whose success can only be determined *in comparison* with socially established criteria.

This should already give us a first indication of why Rousseau, unlike many other thinkers of his time, believed that acting in accordance with the anticipated judgment of our peers represents a potential evil. Rousseau's belief stems from the fact that he regards the adoption of such a social perspective as forcing subjects into a kind of competitive

---

[24] Neuhouser, *Rousseau's Theodicy of Self-Love*, pp. 32–7. See also the remarks on "positional goods" sought for by "inflamed amour propre" in N. J. H. Dent, *Rousseau: An Introduction to His Psychological, Social and Political Theory* (Oxford: Blackwell, 1988), pp. 62ff. On the "comparatism" of "amour propre", see also the highly interesting interpretation given by Barbara Carnevali, *Romantisme et reconnaissance: Figures de la conscience chez Rousseau* (Geneva: Droz, 2012), pp. 28–37.

situation, one in which they feel challenged to prove their abilities according to given social standards and in comparison with their contemporaries. They thus develop an inclination for feigning talents and abilities they do not have. The negative connotation Rousseau bestows on the need for recognition therefore essentially derives from his categorial decision to view the kind of recognition sought for in "amour propre" almost exclusively as the recognition of characteristics that allow a subject to stand out from the crowd.

In no way, however, does this mean that Rousseau sees the compulsion to feign characteristics or abilities which accompanies our craving for social recognition as the primary problem. Although he regards vaingloriousness and braggadocio as being rampant in the Paris of his day,[25] Rousseau is mainly concerned with an entirely different problem, a further consequence which he, astoundingly enough, interprets in line with La Rochefoucauld: The more individuals' need for esteem leads them to display their own advantageous attributes, the more they will be tempted to deceive themselves about their own true personality. After all, when these individuals seek to satisfy their "amour propre", they are not primarily out to convince their peers of their own excellence, but rather their own internalized judge. This results in a kind of internal puzzle, making it impossible for us to recognize the true essence of our own personality. I believe this is the idea at

---

[25] In his *Confessions*, Rousseau reports how "poor Jean-Jacques" suffered in Paris from having to "shine" in the elite circles of the nobility and the rising bourgeoisie in order to gain attention: Jean-Jacques Rousseau, *Confessions* (Oxford: Oxford University Press, 2008), esp. pp. 280–5.

the heart of that famous formulation Rousseau employs to summarize the results of his discourse:

> The savage man lives within himself; social man lives always outside himself; he knows how to live only in the opinion of others, it is, so to speak from their judgement alone that he derives the sense of his own existence.[26]

Rousseau is strongly convinced that the danger of losing one's self as a consequence of "amour propre" lies at the root of everything he has to say in the *Discourse on Inequality* about the social pathologies of his time. Humans in bourgeois society constantly strive to develop attributes that give them a superior social position in the eyes of their internalized observer. Once this "fervent activity"[27] of "amour propre" gets under way, it knows no bounds; its relative character causes every feature that grants distinction to wear out quickly, thus merely leading to further efforts to demonstrate superiority. What counted yesterday as a sign of individual superiority in terms of wealth, power or beauty must be outdone today, leading to an upward spiral in the competition for status in all fields.[28] As we have seen, the theatre merely acts as a forum for this cultural process, strengthening and refining it; Rousseau despises the theatre because it trains citizens to feign characteristics and status markers so convincingly that they themselves can no longer be certain of what their true nature actually is.

Had Rousseau not further refined his theory of recognition, we would be faced with what over eighty years ago Ernst

---

[26] Rousseau, *Discourse on Inequality*, p. 84. [27] Ibid., p. 62.
[28] See Neuhouser, *Rousseau's Theodicy of Self-Love*, p. 75.

Cassirer called *the* "Rousseau problem".[29] We would not know how to bridge the gap between the pessimistic diagnosis in his *Discourse on Inequality* and the more optimistic premises in the *Social Contract* in which he expresses his faith in the capacity of his contemporary citizens for self-determination. Since Cassirer many authors have struggled to grasp this apparent dissonance in Rousseau's writing and have often resigned themselves to emphasizing the irreconcilability of the two works. In his early cultural criticism, Rousseau sees a dependence on public opinion which leads to loss of self, whereas in the *Social Contract* he sees the same humans as being capable of determining their own will.[30] In an attempt to move beyond this unproductive state of research, in 1989 the English Rousseau expert N. J. H. Dent suggested that Rousseau may have made a distinction between "inflamed" and "ordinary" forms of "amour propre". In the *Discourse on Inequality*, we only read of the poisonous forms our need for recognition can take on if we seek to satisfy it under unfavorable social conditions; in the *Social Contract*, by contrast, we read that under the egalitarian conditions of a republic the same need can take on the healthy form of mutual respect.[31] Following Dent's theory, as a number of authors such as Joshua Cohen and Frederick Neuhouser do,[32] we would arrive at a very

---

[29] Ernst Cassirer, *The Question of Jean-Jacques Rousseau* (New Haven: Yale University Press, 1989).

[30] On these interpretive difficulties, see Jean Starobinski, *La transparence et l'obstacle* (Paris: Gallimard, 1971), ch. 2.

[31] Dent, *Rousseau*.

[32] Joshua Cohen, *Rousseau: A Free Community of Equals* (Oxford: Oxford University Press, 2010); Neuhouser, *Rousseau's Theodicy of Self-Love*. On

different interpretation from the one I have offered here. "Amour propre" would then have an entirely different meaning for Rousseau than for his French predecessors, i.e. a psychological mutability or plasticity allowing it to change its form depending on sociocultural conditions. Once society allows all members of society to encounter each other as equals, the evil craving to be viewed as superior or more excellent than others could change into the socially reconcilable need for mutual respect and recognition of one's own autonomy. Indeed, in Rousseau's *Émile*, written seven years after the *Discourse on Inequality*, we find pedagogical measures that could in fact effect such a change in the shape of "amour propre". For instance, he writes that adolescent children could be taught to view other children as beings who also struggle for recognition in order to nip in the bud any desire for status and prestige.[33] And the *Social Contract*, also published in 1762, provides even more evidence that Rousseau assumes "amour propre" to be capable of changing shape depending on the given social order, such that under the right conditions it could even take on the form of respect among equals. This work makes both the entire construction of the social contract as well as the subsequent procedure for determining the "volonté générale" contingent on the

both of these new interpretations of Rousseau, see my essay "Die Entgiftung des Jean-Jacques Rousseau: Neuere Literatur zum Werk des Philosophen", *Deutsche Zeitschrift für Philosophie*, vol. 4 (2012), pp. 611–32.

[33] Jean-Jacques Rousseau, *Émile or: On Education* (New York: Basic Books, 1979), p. 245; see also Neuhouser, *Rousseau's Theodicy of Self-Love*, pp. 170–83.

willingness of subjects to recognize each other's autonomy, thus appearing to eliminate, at least for the time being, any need for superiority, privilege and individual grandeur.[34] If we summarize the intent of both of these works, we obtain a more complex picture of Rousseau's understanding of "amour propre". It represents a need arising in the course of human socialization, a need to count as beings who fundamentally deserve respect in the (internalized) eyes of other members of society, and thus have a social right to exist. This originally innocent desire does not become a poisonous arrow in the heart of humans unless social conditions or improper education deprive them of recognizing that all other individuals are engaged in the same struggle for social respect. Under these conditions the socially compatible longing for recognition turns into the fierce, unchecked desire to appear especially commendable or excellent. In short, everything Rousseau has to say about the danger of loss of self due to our dependence on others' judgment would only apply to societies in which there are no possibilities for satisfying the elementary need for social involvement and integration.[35]

In the last step of my discussion of Rousseau's work, however, I want to show that this is in fact not true, and that Rousseau retained his reservations about "amour propre" throughout his life. To do so, I will first have to take a new

---

[34] "Of the Social Contract", in *The Social Contract and Other Later Political Writings*, ed. Victor Gourevitch (New York: Cambridge University Press, 1997), pp. 3–150; see also Cohen, *Rousseau*, pp. 32–59; Neuhouser, *Rousseau's Theodicy of Self-Love*, pp. 205–17.

[35] This is the argument presented e.g. by Joshua Cohen (in *Rousseau*) and Frederick Neuhouser (in *Rousseau's Theodicy of Self-Love*).

and brief look at the *Social Contract*, for this work contains a few lines of argumentation I believe prove that the author retains his skepticism about a need for recognition that has become part of humans' "second nature". First, there is Rousseau's odd tendency to conceive of the procedure for agreeing upon a common will, the "volonté générale", as an act which each individual performs on its own in a kind of silent conversion.[36] As much as the text warns us not to confuse the general will with the mere addition of the wills of all individual citizens, it says very little about the kind of deliberations that would mediate between these individual wills. Instead we find numerous remarks which give the impression that Rousseau sought to ensure that one individual's will-formation will not become dependent on that of another. Because any exchange with others might cause an individual subject to deceive itself about its own "true" aims and intentions, each subject should form its opinion as independently as possible.[37] Once Rousseau can no longer avoid treating the sovereign as a collective, he transfers this monological conception to the thinking of a large group, also conceiving of the latter as a kind of unified ego[38] with a single opinion, thus appearing to exclude any dissenting voices. Rousseau characteristically forbids the formation of factions

---

[36] See the formulations in *Social Contract*, Book 1, ch. 8. See also Jürgen Habermas, *Between Facts and Norms* (Cambridge, MA: MIT Press, 1992), pp. 94–103.

[37] This also includes Rousseau's notion that at the conclusion of the social contract, each individual "makes a contract with himself, so to say" (Rousseau, *Social Contract*, p. 51).

[38] Rousseau himself speaks of a "common ego", p. 50.

in the development of the common will, regarding them as a threat to the latter's unity.[39] In the first instance this only means that there is little evidence to support the assumption that Rousseau believed in the epistemic fruitfulness of discourse; instead we get the clear impression that he still believes that individual subjects – be they individuals or collectives – should form their wills independently of others.

This impression becomes even stronger once we turn to Rousseau's work following the publication of the *Social Contract*. It would certainly not be wrong to claim that after 1762, the old pairing of a striving for recognition and a loss of self once again comes to the fore.[40] Rousseau seems fixated on determining how to experience what is truly authentic about one's own personality; his thinking becomes ever more peculiar. The most serious obstacle to this experience continues to be our habit of viewing ourselves from the perspective of those whom we seek to convince of our merits and valuable qualities. With the question of how to live an authentic life, the issue that defined his discourse on inequality reappears in Rousseau's later, more autobiographical writings in a different form: If we are constantly "living in the opinion of others", because the passion of "amour propre" has become our second nature, how can we ever find our way back to ourselves, to the core of our own unique personality? In this reformulation of Rousseau's old problem, the latter's epistemic connotations play a much stronger role. Whereas it was previously unclear whether the dangers of a craving for social recognition are moral or cognitive, it now becomes obvious

---

[39] Ibid., p. 60. [40] Starobinski, *La transparence et l'obstacle*, pp. 268–98.

that Rousseau has in mind a cognitive difficulty, the problem of adequately recognizing our own self.

Already in *Rousseau, Judged by Jean-Jacques*, published in 1782, five years after the philosopher's death,[41] and despite his angry reckoning with what he took to be an attack on his reputation, Rousseau subtly deals with the problem of how we can find our own unique personality regardless of others' varying opinions about ourselves; due to our culturally acquired disposition to judge our own behavior from the perspective of others, we have trouble sweeping aside internalized judgments and arriving at an adequate judgment of our own true self. The cognitive problem Rousseau addresses here has two sides, depending on our respective stance. Either we feign a kind of excellence we do not truly possess, in which case we are easily seduced by the ideal image we have produced of ourselves, or public opinion is wrong from the start about our attributes, in which case it is nearly impossible to get rid of such errors, because we have made them our own and cannot find any cognitive purchase without them. In both cases we are so tangled up in others' ascriptions that we can no longer get to the core of our own being – hence Rousseau's desperate comment at the start of his emotional text: "Should he speak of himself with praise that is merited but generally denied?"[42]

What clearly appears to be an epistemic problem of self-recognition reveals in hindsight what Rousseau took to

---

[41] Jean-Jacques Rousseau, *Rousseau, Judge of Jean-Jacques*, in *The Collected Wrtings of Rousseau*, vol. 1 (Hanover, NH: Dartmouth College Press, 2012).

[42] Ibid., p. 6.

be the evil of "amour propre" from the very beginning. There are in principle two different dangers involved in desiring to appear "good" or "excellent" according to prevailing standards. There is the "political and moral" danger that we will end up in an unjust position in the social hierarchy, or there is the epistemic danger of no longer being able to break through the veil of public opinion, thus permanently concealing our "true" essence. Certainly, these are abstract alternatives, since in social reality both of them are generally closely related, making an unjust status often the result of a public misjudgment of a person's true merits. But depending on our interest and our diagnostic attentiveness, we can emphasize either side of this danger. Rousseau, who is initially uncertain about which is the greater threat, ultimately arrives at the conclusion that the epistemic danger represents the truly dramatic challenge. Our dependence on social recognition is so harmful and deserves our full philosophical attention because of the resulting uncertainty about our true individual nature. He thereby reaffirms at a new and theoretically advanced level the suspicion of the French moralists that the craving for recognition constantly threatens to engender a false self-understanding. Even if Rousseau, like La Rochefoucauld or Montaigne, does not use the term "recognition" explicitly, the ambivalence of the French term "re-connaissance" as a cognitive or moral act is always at issue.

The end of Rousseau's lifelong discussion of the issue of "amour propre" can be described in a few words. In the same year as his *Rousseau, Judged by Jean-Jacques* was published (1782), his *Reveries of a Solitary Walker* were also made available to the public in Lausanne.[43] As if to underline the particular danger of our need for recognition, Rousseau beseeches the reader to follow the path of self-recognition in as much isolation as possible. Only when we no longer care what other people think of us and which of our abilities they admire will we be able to recognize our true characteristics and our true concerns. It is thus only logical that Rousseau describes in his famous fifth walk how the silent observation of nature represents the ideal way to recognize adequately our own, unadulterated self: Because nature can neither speak nor cast judgment, it gives no fuel to the stirring of our "amour propre" and allows us to recognize ourselves without concern for our social reputation.[44]

Before I further discuss the fate of the idea of recognition in the French context following Rousseau, I would like to briefly summarize the results of the first step of my reconstruction. Both La Rochefoucauld and Rousseau believe, though the latter does so much more strongly, that the

---

[43] Jean-Jacques Rousseau, *The Reveries of the Solitary Walker*, in *The Collected Writings of Rousseau*, vol. 8 (Hanover, NH: Dartmouth College, 2000).

[44] Ibid., pp. 49–56. A wonderful interpretation of this key chapter is found in Heinrich Meier, *Über das Glück des philosophischen Lebens: Reflexionen zu Rousseaus Rêveries in zwei Büchern* (Munich: Beck, 2011). On the entire subject of Rousseau's stoic withdrawal from society as a forum for "amour propre", see also Starobinski, *Rousseau*, esp. pp. 56–74. A comparable proposal that a peaceful, calm relationship-to-self is best served by abandoning all relations of recognition can also be found, though without reference to Rousseau, in Ernst Tugendhat, *Egocentricity and Mysticism* (New York: Columbia University Press, 2016).

dependence of our passion for "amour propre" on the esteem of others is highly problematic in a primarily epistemic sense. Whereas the French moralists argue that this dependence produces a tendency to feign virtues we do not possess, thus rendering us incapable of distinguishing between our feigned and our real self, Rousseau's concerns are much more profound. He wonders what it means at all to judge ourselves from the perspective of others. Throughout his life he has trouble giving a clear answer to this question. On the one hand, he is concerned about the danger of a loss of certainty about what is right for us ("amour de soi"); on the other hand, he sees the chance to attain an egalitarian consciousness of mutual dependencies and obligations. In the *Social Contract* he seems, at least temporarily, convinced that the cultural need for "amour propre" enables us to open ourselves to the views of others, which in turn allows us to respect each other as equals. In the end, however, and as I have shown, this belief is outweighed by his skepticism about the effects of our "amour propre". As Rousseau grows older, the belief already outlined in his *Discourse on Inequality*, which is that our compulsive attachment to others' judgment prevents us from arriving at a true understanding of the authentic, unique core of our personality, becomes more resolute. The reasons he offers for this concern in his later works are complex and extremely subtle. I will nevertheless briefly summarize them here, for in them we find some of the doubts that will later reappear in French thought in an altered form and under completely different circumstances.

As we have seen, Rousseau initially claims that the need for "amour propre" compels us to judge ourselves from the perspective of our peers, rather than from the internal perspective of an isolated yet self-certain actor. As soon as we enter a sufficiently large community, we will seek to appear in an advantageous light, thus forcing ourselves to act in accordance with the criteria for how others evaluate the characteristics that reveal themselves through our actions. This claim suffices to qualify Rousseau as a theorist of recognition, for he characterizes socialized human individuals as beings who can only view themselves as subjects with unique attributes if they are confirmed as such by their peers or find the latter's recognition. It remains unclear, however, what we mean when we speak of "confirmation" or "recognition" in this context. Normally we would say that such a reaction demands that we pay respect to the recognized subject in a manner that is adequate to the characteristics to be confirmed or recognized. At this point, however, Rousseau appears to vacillate, incapable of deciding whether recognition entails a cognitive judgment of approval or an accordance of moral respect. He clearly implies that subjects are primarily interested in having their feigned or actual characteristics adequately noticed, thus merely cognitively confirmed. So we could also say that the struggle for recognition, which, according to Rousseau, has been gaining intensity ever since the emergence of "amour propre", primarily consists in competing efforts to convince others of our own presumed or real attributes. To express the matter more clearly, individuals do not struggle to attain each other's moral respect or the granting of a "normative status", but rather the cognitive verification or affirmation of the characteristics they display to their peers.

On the basis of this one-sided, cognitivist view of our intentions whenever we seek to act in accordance with the judgments of others, Rousseau believes he is justified in drawing the conclusion that was the focus of my characterization of his theory of recognition: because subjects are driven by their "amour propre" to prove their feigned or real characteristics, they will eventually fail to recognize themselves. With every attempt to prove their worth they will become increasingly uncertain about who in fact has the authority to define their attributes and abilities – public opinion or themselves, to whom they likewise feel accountable? On the basis of this epistemic confusion, Rousseau develops the inner drama that takes up so much space in his later, more autobiographical writings: Individual subjects, torn between their own judgment of their personal identity and that of others, ultimately fail to know who they really are.

Although this issue – both the ideal and the questionable, fleeting nature of individual authenticity – stood in the center of Rousseau's later works, it initially drew little attention.[45] The concept of "amour propre" ceased to be a major category of French cultural and social life at the conclusion of the eighteenth century; it would also virtually cease to be viewed as a technological means of social self-understanding, despite the fact that the negative meaning of the expression would still remain for a time, for example, in

[45] On the contemporary significance of these terms, see Alessandro Ferrara, *Modernity and Authenticity: A Study of the Social and Ethical Thought of Jean-Jacques Rousseau* (New York: SUNY Press, 1992).

Stendhal's frequent use of the terms "vanité" and "orgueil".[46] More importantly, however, the political debates in the run-up to the French Revolution caused entirely different elements of Rousseau's work to come to the fore. For at least a century, the *Social Contract* would determine the philosopher's view of the political and scientific public. This period witnessed a general decline of interest in relationships of interpersonal recognition; the dominance of the democratic challenge and subsequently of the social question would shift the focus to issues of social policy, be it in Auguste Comte's theory of order, early socialism or the discipline of sociology founded by Durkheim.[47] Of course, the question of who owes whom what kind of recognition in society and what that in turn means for the individual still played a role for this type of theoretical discussion; the leading French thinkers of the

---

[46] See again Fuchs, *Entfremdung und Narzißmus*, p. 293. In Kant's writings on the philosophy of history, Rousseau's concept of "amour propre" is revived at the end of the eighteenth century, though not in the French terminology. On the significance of the idea of "amour propre" in the work of Kant, see Yirmiyahu Yovel, *Kant and the Philosophy of History* (Princeton: Princeton University Press, 1989), Part II. We could also refer, alongside Stendhal, to Balzac, who in the first part of his otherwise grandiloquent story *The Girl With the Golden Eyes* offers a quite ingenious sociological analysis of the "selfishness" of the struggle for "money, fame and pleasure" at all levels of 1830s Paris: Honoré de Balzac, *The Girl With the Golden Eyes* (London: Melville House, 2011). Here we also find direct references to La Rochefoucauld and Rousseau, which demonstrate just how familiar Balzac was with their works.

[47] On these far-reaching developments, see the interesting considerations presented by Raymond Aron, "The Sociologists and the Revolution of 1848", in *Main Currents in Sociological Thought*, vol. 1 (London: Routledge Classics, 2018), pp. 248–78.

time, however, either approached the issue of social integration from the perspective of the state or employed the idea of a collective consciousness without taking any notice of a connection to mutual recognition in everyday life. Durkheim, who was aware that social integration requires a whole network of various different relations of recognition, represents the sole exception.[48]

Although the problem posed by Rousseau with regard to interpersonal relations hardly played any role in French thought for a long period of time, it would re-emerge with all the more force in the course of the twentieth century once positivist and spiritualist currents had begun to ebb and a new philosophical movement had started to emerge. French thinkers, more than anywhere else in Europe, soon picked up on Husserl's method of describing how consciousness constitutes the world and applied it to a number of various theoretical undertakings previously ignored by the philosophical mainstream.[49] It would not be long before the relation of

---

[48] Émile Durkheim, *Physik der Sitten und des Rechts: Vorlesungen zur Soziologie der Moral* (Frankfurt: Suhrkamp, 1999). Marcel Mauss' groundbreaking study on social reciprocity in gift exchange (Mauss, *The Gift* (Chicago: HAU Books, 2016)) launched an intellectual development in France in the course of which questions of mutual recognition are directly addressed. See Marcel Hénaff, *The Price of Truth: Gift, Money, and Philosophy* (Stanford: Stanford University Press, 2010), esp. ch. 4. See also my own discussion of the issue in Axel Honneth, "Vom Gabentausch zur sozialen Anerkennung: Unstimmigkeiten in der Sozialtheorie von Marcel Hénaff", *WestEnd*, 1 (2010), pp. 99–101.

[49] On the history of twentieth-century French philosophy, see Gary Gutting, *French Philosophy in the Twentieth Century* (Cambridge: Cambridge University Press, 2001).

the subject to its peers, examined by Rousseau, would once again become an object of philosophical study. Alongside Gabriel Marcel with his predominantly Catholic leanings, Maurice Merleau-Ponty and Jean-Paul Sartre would take the lead in addressing the issue of how one subject's relation to other subjects can be understood from the phenomenological perspective of the individual.[50] Of these three philosophers, however, Sartre alone would manage to put his stamp on the *zeitgeist* of an entire epoch and make existentialism the core of its new self-understanding. A major reason for the enormous and rapid effect of Sartre's theory is the fact that Sartre, like Rousseau, takes an extremely dark view of our dependence on others. The theoretical conditions under which he develops this negative view of recognition, however, are so different from those of the Genevan philosopher that a brief explanation is needed to bridge this broad gap.

In his lifelong attempt to explore the dangers and opportunities of bourgeois society, Rousseau naively assumed that he could distinguish between natural predispositions and secondary, acquired passions. By employing a kind of philosophical anthropology, Rousseau examined the latter, culturally acquired need – the "amour propre" that causes us to become dependent on others – in order to determine whether this need was a blessing or a curse both on our social life and on the individual. Two hundred years later, Sartre would not even dream of studying the nature of human needs in such an

---

[50] Maurice Merleau-Ponty, *Phenomenology of Perception* (London: Routledge, 2013), pp. 148–53; Jean-Paul Sartre, *Being and Nothingness* (New York: Washington Square Press, 1984), esp. Part III.

objectivist fashion; having been influenced by philosophy's critical turn and raised on Husserl's phenomenology, Sartre was convinced that everything we are and can be is only comprehensible from the perspective of a self-conscious subject. In *Being and Nothingness*, he therefore pursues an entirely different strategy for grasping intersubjective encounters. He does not inquire into the potential consequences of this human need for our lives, but undertakes a phenomenological investigation into whether and to what extent the subject's existential state changes once it encounters another subject. Given all these significant differences between these two thinkers, it is astounding – and decisive for our purposes – that Sartre's analysis of intersubjectivity arrives at a result that is perhaps not identical, but quite similar, to that of Rousseau.

Sartre begins his investigation by recalling briefly the results of his previous analysis, according to which a subject, prior to encountering others, finds itself in an ontological state he terms "être pour soi" ("being-for-itself"). This means that unlike all other beings, whose characteristics are fixed and thus impenetrable, solid and self-contained ("être en soi"),[51] humans are always faced with a future whose possibilities are open, and must therefore constantly redefine themselves through their choices.[52] Sartre owes much of his description of this specifically human freedom, the "being-for-itself", to Heidegger's famous analysis of "Dasein" ("being-in-the-world") in *Being and Time*,[53] although Sartre occasionally attempts to conceal

---

[51] Sartre, *Being and Nothingness*, pp. 24–30. [52] Ibid., Part II, ch. 1.
[53] Martin Heidegger, *Being and Time* (Oxford: Blackwell, 1962).

this fact by making a few minimal modifications. After he describes the subject as experiencing its own existence as a constant redefinition of possibilities, Part III of his book begins with an encounter with another subject – which in turn must, of course, possess the characteristics of being "pour soi". We can already gain a vague sense of how this encounter will end, but before it does, for a fraction of a second something takes place for which Sartre uses the Hegelian term "recognition": the moment the first subject, with whose existential situation we have become familiar, feels itself observed by another subject, it must suddenly acquire perfect certainty about its "being-with-others", a certainty in which each side must also feel recognized as an individual "for-itself".[54] Of course, this ontological realization that I exist among others and that we always already "recognize" each other as free subjects is supposed to take place solely in this brief moment, before the consequences of the first subject's encounter come to pass. After all, as soon as this first subject feels itself observed by another subject in the process of a given activity (Sartre uses the example of peering through a keyhole),[55] it will suddenly feel itself robbed of its entire "being-for-itself". The observation of the other inevitably commits the subject to certain characteristics, thus turning it into a being "an sich", to an "être-en-soi". According to Sartre, the drama of the subject that experiences itself as free consists in the fact that it can only

---

[54] Sartre, *Being and Nothingness*, Part III, ch. 1, sec. IV ("The Look"), esp. pp. 345–50.

[55] Ibid., pp. 347ff.

experience the other as a free, undetermined subject with an open future if it reciprocally and simultaneously sees itself reduced to a mere thing.

We need not concern ourselves with Sartre's conclusion that this first encounter leads to a permanent conflict in which subjects endlessly restrict each other to specific reifying characteristics.[56] Although this image of society, for which Sartre famously employs a metaphor in which "the others" are "hell",[57] contributed a great deal to the sudden success of *Being and Nothingness*, for our purposes it suffices to note how Sartre describes the first encounter between these two subjects. Nor must we address the fact that Sartre also claims to have solved once and for all the old problem of how to prove the existence of "other minds".[58] Although this is certainly significant in the history of philosophy and can be regarded as a groundbreaking proposal, it contributes little to our understanding of the specific nature of his concept of recognition. We need only note that Sartre assumes that the experience of being recognized by others necessarily implies our failure to recognize our own "being-for-itself" and thus our own freedom. I have already mentioned his argument for this surprising claim, but for the purpose of further clarification I will restate it in a somewhat different fashion: Sartre believes that once a subject experiences itself as being viewed – or later: addressed[59] – by another subject, it become aware

---

[56] Ibid., Part III, ch. 3.
[57] Jean-Paul Sartre, *No Exit,* in *No Exit and Three Other Plays* (New York: Vintage Books, 1955), p. 47.
[58] Sartre, *Being and Nothingness*, Part III, pp. 303–14.   [59] Ibid., pp. 513ff.

that it is a "being-for-itself" among many others. This is because, we might add, the subject would be incapable of understanding the other's view of itself if it did not simultaneously understand itself and the other viewer (or speaker) as intentional, and thus free, beings. In the moment in which all this takes place, Sartre claims that the same subject experiences itself as a mere being "an sich" for others, as a self-contained being, because the gaze of the other ascribes to it certain fixed characteristics. Because these two experiences take place in one and the same moment, Sartre concludes that being observed or spoken to necessarily entails both recognition and reification, the affirmation of our own "being-for-itself" and the failure to recognize it as such.

At this point a further affinity between Sartre's and Rousseau's idea of recognition emerges. Both assume, though for different reasons, that the experience of being recognized has a negative, undesired consequence. For Rousseau, it creates uncertainty about one's own self, and for Sartre, it leads to a loss of being-for-itself and thus freedom. For the Genevan philosopher the public affirmation of our own supposed or true characteristics can lead to uncertainty about which attributes we truly possess, while for Sartre the gaze or the speaking of the other to us necessarily ascribes to us fixed characteristics, thus depriving us of the chance to redefine ourselves constantly. This in turn reveals a second, more profound affinity: both Rousseau and Sartre grasp the type of recognition accorded to individuals as a kind of propositional cognition or factual claim, rather than as an act of moral consideration or respect. I have already shown this cognitivist one-sidedness in Rousseau's implicit discussion of recognition, and I still need to do so for Sartre's use of the term. This is much easier than one might think, for Sartre's very description of the "gaze" already makes such a restriction apparent. Surprisingly enough, he does not define the gaze normatively, as being "evil", "encouraging", "indifferent", or "punishing"; instead he characterizes it as a mere cognition of the existence of another person, which causes the latter to lose its being-for-itself. For Sartre the only relevant issue here is that a previously pre-reflexive individual suddenly is forced to grasp itself as the addressee of another intentional being and thus as just one subject among many. Sartre completely ignores whether this individual can feel respected or vilified, morally respected or injured by the other, which only confirms the assumptions of earlier commentators[60] that Sartre reduces intersubjective encounters to a purely ontological occurrence in which a subject, depending on its relation to the other, can only be "für sich" or "an sich". As a consequence, the recognition that somehow takes place between these two protagonists necessarily has the form of an ascription or cognition of ontological characteristics. Like Rousseau, Sartre views recognition primarily as a cognitive act in which we take note of personal attributes, an act that thus has no moral qualities.

These astounding commonalities certainly should not move us to equate Rousseau's and Sartre's approaches to

---

[60] First indications in this direction can be found in Maurice Merleau-Ponty, *Phenomenology of Perception*, p. 461–4; see also Michael Theunissen, *Der Andere: Studien zur Sozialontologie der Gegenwart* (Berlin and New York: de Gruyter, 1977), Part 1, ch. VI.

the phenomenon of recognition. Two hundred years of groundbreaking philosophical change lies between them, a fact made apparent by their diametrically opposed methods. Rousseau describes recognition from the anthropological perspective of an observer who claims to recognize therein certain psychological regularities or distinctive features, whereas Sartre takes up the perspective of a self-reflecting subject in order to explore what occurs once this subject encounters another subject. Nevertheless, the degree to which both thinkers agree that intersubjective encounters necessarily entail a kind of self-loss on the part of the recognized subject is highly remarkable.

Even if we take into consideration my account of La Rochefoucauld, we still cannot draw the conclusion that French thought tends toward a negative understanding of recognition. Thus far we have only gathered a few indications that ever since the seventeenth century, prominent French philosophers have had doubts about the ethical value of intersubjectivity or interpersonal communication. We will find further support for this claim, however, once we continue to follow the development of French thought after Sartre and refocus on the discussion of the issue of recognition. Surprisingly, the philosophical current that rebelled against Sartre's phenomenology in the 1960s and quickly managed to break its domination, i.e. so-called post-structuralism, in fact retained the negative accentuation of recognition.

At first sight, it might seem odd to associate this new philosophical movement with the topic of recognition at all. After all, post-structuralists explicitly sought to destroy the prevalent notion in contemporary philosophy of a transparent, world-constituting subject and replace it with the idea that anonymous social or cognitive structures are what perform such constitutive acts of creating meaning.[61] So how could it be possible within the framework of such a radically transformed paradigm to ascribe an essential, perhaps even decisive, role to interpersonal encounters in the process of social reproduction? The problem disappears, however, once we realize that we do not necessarily have to understand recognition as a concrete interaction between subjects; it can also be conceived of as an effect of whole systems. In this case, "recognition" would mean a bundle of systematically organized practices through which, with the help of acting subjects, certain attributes are ascribed to individuals or groups. We saw tendencies of such an anonymous or structuralist manner of speaking in the work of Sartre, who, for example, claims that language as a whole or the entirely anonymous gaze of the "other" can manage to address a subject as a specifically constituted individual.[62] Moreover, the post-structuralist work of Louis Althusser and Jacques Lacan, both of whom employ the idea of recognition in crucial parts of their work, merely radicalizes Sartre's own thought – a fact of which these authors themselves were perhaps not aware. I will return briefly to this last turn in the development of the issue of recognition in French thought in the conclusion.

---

[61] See Gutting, *French Philosophy*, Part III; see also Vincent Descombes, *Modern French Philosophy* (Cambridge: Cambridge University Press, 1980).

[62] Sartre, *Being and Nothingness*, Part III, pp. 486f.: "The Other is always there, present and experienced as the one who gives to language its meaning" (p. 487).

The radicalizing step by which Althusser and Lacan distance themselves from Sartre's ideas obviously consists – in keeping with their post-structuralist premises – in fundamentally denying the existence of a pre-existent self-reflexive subject. Whereas Sartre sought to understand what it could mean phenomenologically for a subject's "being-for-itself" to become conscious of another subject, his two successors proceed in the opposite direction, asking how a given individual becomes a subject convinced of its own existence and its own reflexivity by virtue of the "interpellation" of the other. For Althusser and Lacan, therefore, the kind of "recognition" they speak of with explicit reference to Hegel must have an entirely different function compared to all the other French theories we have dealt with thus far. Unlike Rousseau, for whom recognition consists in the esteem which a subject desires to receive from others, and unlike Sartre, who defines it as the inner experience of being recognized by another subject, here recognition denotes a mechanism of ascribing. This mechanism continuously constitutes subjectivity, i.e. a subject equipped with self-consciousness. In the work of Althusser, this project develops into a theory of ideology which seeks to explain why humans are generally willing to act in a way that serves to reproduce the dominant social order. He claims that this "willing servitude" is due to a series of state institutions whose ritual practices ensure that members of society are "recognized" precisely as they are supposed to be in accordance with the order of social domination.[63] "Recognition" thus entails that

---

[63] Louis Althusser, *On the Reproduction of Capitalism: Ideology and Ideological State Apparatuses* (London: Verso, 2014), pp. 171–207. See also the fantastic interpretation by Kristina Leopold, to whom I owe very

a bundle of state-organized rituals addresses subjects, makes demands on them and gives them behavioral reminders until they adopt the characteristics that have already been ascribed to them – though how they do so remains unclear. According to Althusser, once a subject has internalized these characteristics, it will conform to society's demands while remaining convinced that it is doing so of its own free will. It is easy to see that, after a long process of emptying and thinning, this interpretation robs recognition of any remaining moral elements. In the work of Althusser, this complex and enigmatic concept does not even represent a cognitive act or the recognition of personal attributes; it merely denotes the ascription of demanded characteristics for the purpose of stabilizing a system of domination.

Roughly the same applies to Jacques Lacan, who at certain points in his psychoanalytical theory also employs the term "recognition", with which he had become familiar through Alexandre Kojève's famous lectures on Hegel.[64] He thereby means little more than the ascription of personal characteristics, although he views the system of language as the source of such attributions. Lacan develops this thought in connection with his explanation of the processes of socialization through which

much, but with whom, however, I ultimately cannot agree: Kristina Leopold, *Ambivalente Anerkennung: Immanente Kritik und die Herausforderung ideologischer Anerkennungsverhältnisse* (Dissertation, Goethe Universität, Frankfurt 2016), ch. 4.

[64] Alexandre Kojève, *Introduction to the Reading of Hegel: Lectures on the Phenomenology of Spirit* (Ithaca, NY: Cornell University Press, 1980). On the significance of Hegel's idea of recognition for Lacan's psychoanalysis, see Hermann Lang, *Die Sprache und das Unbewußte: Jacques Lacans Grundlegung der Psychoanalyse* (Frankfurt: Suhrkamp, 1973), chs 1 and 4, sec. 3.

small children are integrated into the prevailing social order.[65] The child's desire to be "recognized by the other" is accommodated by the mother's attempt to satisfy the vital needs of her child, thereby inevitably employing expressions and phrases from the symbolic order of her cultural environment. This introduces a foreign element into the formation of the child's drives, compelling the latter to articulate its desires exclusively by means of the language the mother uses to symbolize the child's silent demands. The consequence of this early "division" of the child's psyche into a communicative and a mute part represents in Lacan's view a primitive form of self-alienation affecting all humans in the same way.[66] Here we see the same motif we encountered in French thought starting with Rousseau, which is that recognition and self-loss have a common origin, though under entirely different philosophical premises: the human subject, constitutively dependent on being recognized by others, loses itself in others' ascriptions and thus suffers a "division" of its I into a conscious part and an inaccessible part.

At the same time, however, Lacan's writings on child socialization show that he regards the concept of recognition as a mere act in which one subject accords certain attributes to

[65] Jacques Lacan, *The Language of the Self: The Function of Language in Psychoanalysis* (Baltimore: Johns Hopkins University Press, 1998). The model for this "self-loss" of the subject in the other, upon whose recognition it remains dependent, is for Lacan the experience of small children of seeing the imaginary image of their unity or entirety in the mirror. See Lacan, "The Mirror Stage as Formative of the I Function as Revealed in Psycholanalytic Experience", in *Ecrits* (New York and London: Norton, 2006), pp. 75–81. On this motive see also the early essay by Althusser, *Writings on Psychoanalysis: Freud and Lacan* (New York: Columbia University Press, 1996).

[66] See Lang, *Die Sprache und das Unbewußte*, ch. 5, sec. 2.

another subject. A mother's attempts to satisfy the needs of her child thus not only appear to lack any moral component of love or resonance of individuality, but also any cognitive effort to understand the personal characteristics of her child. Here, "recognition" ultimately signifies an unwilling projection of attributes determined by the prevailing symbolic order onto the helpless child. Like Althusser, Lacan also defines recognition as little more than an active, repeated mode of ascribing social characteristics or features that serve to uphold the prevailing order.

I do not want to give a definitive answer to the question of whether these concluding remarks on post-structuralism suffice to prove the claim that French thought generally accords a negative meaning to interpersonal recognition. At any rate I have found enough evidence to dare to make the claim that French philosophy has a tendency to view intersubjectivity as a problem rather than as an opportunity for individual subjects. Certainly, there are a few French thinkers who saw matters differently and thus pose an exception to the rule, for example, Durkheim and Mauss, whom I mentioned earlier, as well as Montesquieu.[67] Nevertheless, on the whole we find sufficient evidence to claim a certain cultural bias. In my attempt to

---

[67] Montesquieu virtually inverts Rousseau's skepticism in the Second Discourse: "The more communicative a people are the more easily they change their habits, because each is in a greater degree a spectacle to the other, and the singularities of individuals are better observed" (Montesquieu, *The Spirit of Laws* (New York: Hafner, 1949), p. 295). On Montaigne's more complicated view of recognition, though not dissimilar to that of La Rochefoucauld, see the helpful study by Oliver Guerrier, *Rencontre et reconnaissance: Les "Essais" ou le jeu du hasard et de la vérité* (Paris: Classiques Garnier, 2016), esp. pp. 213–60.

uncover the reasons for this negative accentuation of recognition in French thought, I have encountered two issues that, for the time being, we must treat with great caution: first, the linguistic finding that the French term "reconnaissance" does not clearly distinguish between an epistemic and a moral act – a fact that was insignificant when it came to La Rochefoucauld and Rousseau, because neither of them used the term "reconnaissance" in any systematic manner; second, the sociohistorical presumption that in France, the social conflict over symbolic distinction due to the centralized organization of the country played a much greater role in everyday life, which could partially help to explain the negative connotation of our dependence on others. If public insignia such as clothing style, behavior and consumption ultimately decide an individual's position or rank in the social hierarchy, this might certainly lead to constant conflicts over the value of such means of outward expression and suspicion of the symbolic intentions of others. I hope to gain more clarity about the causes of the negative connotation of intersubjectivity in French thought by contrasting this tradition with that of British thought, in which the idea of recognition has always featured entirely different associations and the development of which would take an entirely different course.

3

From Hume to Mill
Recognition and Self-Control

By asking how the idea of interpersonal recognition emerged and developed in British thought, we cross not only into new territory in the history of ideas, but also into an entirely different political and cultural space. Social philosophy in seventeenth- and eighteenth-century France might have been largely concerned with the issue of social rank and the attendant conflicts, but this was certainly not the case in contemporary Great Britain. If social and political philosophy was faced with a major social challenge at all, then it was the gradual intrusion of instrumental and economic modes of behavior into a public life traditionally protected by moral principles. The significance of this experience of an impending commercialization of society for the English-speaking culture of early modernity can be seen in the wide-ranging discourse in literature and philosophy over the course of three centuries on a newly emergent entity: the self-interested economic subject.[1] The debate began, after a few false starts, in the Elizabethan era at the turn of the seventeenth century, when increased flows of

---

[1] Laurenz Volkmann, *Homo oeconomicus: Studien zur Modellierung eines neuen Menschenbildes in der englischen Literatur vom Mittelalter bis zum 18. Jahrhundert* (Heidelberg: Winter, 2003).

capital led to the rapid growth of England's domestic and foreign markets, thus giving rise to a capitalist mentality throughout the country. There were plenty of indications of pervasive commercialization, from the transformation of traditional agriculture into a market-based economy emphasizing advances in productivity, up to the increasing use of land for industrial purposes and the rapid concentration of world trade in the metropolis of London. In the dramas of Christopher Marlowe, William Shakespeare and Ben Jonson, audiences were presented with symbolic dramatizations of the potential consequences of this rapid expansion of capitalist forms.[2] It was feared that egotism and self-interest would eventually undermine all traditional moral obligations, replacing them with merely calculating forms of behavior. It did not take long for these initial concerns to evolve into a heated discussion about whether the pursuit of pure self-interest would turn out to be generally advantageous or disadvantageous to social well-being. The citizen comedies of Middleton or Rowley caricatured this new, profit-oriented social character enough to make it unrecognizable, while the bourgeois-moralistic plays of Steele or Addison took a more cautious approach toward its defense.[3]

In hindsight, this debate made its most indelible impression on the English-speaking philosophy of the seventeenth and eighteenth centuries, which was largely dominated

---

[2] See Robert Weimann, *Drama und Wirklichkeit in der Shakespearezeit: Ein Beitrag zur Entwicklungsgeschichte des elisabethanischen Theaters* (Halle: Niemeyer, 1958).

[3] See Volkmann, *Homo oeconomicus*, chs 3.6 and 5.2.

by the search for the roots of human morality – either in self-interest or in the natural concern for the well-being of others. On the one side of this intense philosophical debate, the disciples of Thomas Hobbes followed their predecessor in arguing that humans always act out of self-interest and have no predisposition toward socially benevolent behavior. On the other side, the followers of Hugo Grotius assumed humans to have a social capacity that enabled them to show moral concern for the interests of their fellow humans.[4] This controversy reached a boiling point in 1723, when Bernard Mandeville published the third, expanded edition of his *Fable of the Bees*, where we find the famous dispute between "private vices" and "public benefits".[5] This work forced a definitive split between the two sides, as the author makes a number of jabs at Lord Shaftesbury, claiming that the increase of human well-being can only be attained through a politically shrewd arrangement of private, egotistical calculations of utility. These odes to the beneficial effects of self-interest led to a philosophical counter-movement in eighteenth-century England, and thus to the emergence of an idea of recognition strongly opposed to French mistrust in human intersubjectivity. The pioneer of this notion of recognition is David Hume, while Adam Smith would become its central proponent and John Stuart Mill a late, liberal representative.

---

[4] On this discussion see David Fate Norton, "Hume, Human Nature, and the Foundation of Morality", in *The Cambridge Companion to Hume* (Cambridge: Cambridge University Press, 1993), pp. 148–81, esp. pp. 149–55.

[5] Bernard Mandeville, *The Fable of the Bees* (London: Penguin, 1989).

Whereas in seventeenth- and eighteenth-century France the concept of "amour propre" would become a vehicle for reflecting on human intersubjectivity, the concept of "sympathy" would play a similar role in contemporary England. Unlike the concept of "amour propre" in France, however, the term "sympathy" had an entirely positive connotation, revealing the extent of the difference between these two countries in terms of the accents they lent to the term "recognition". The revaluation of the status of intersubjective relations in England began with the writings of Anthony Ashley-Cooper, the third Earl of Shaftesbury, who near the end of the seventeenth century objected to the moral skepticism of his day by claiming that humans are naturally social beings, constantly concerned with the general well-being. As Shaftesbury writes in his critique of Hobbes, he is convinced that this natural "sensus communis" equips us with a moral sensibility for the fate of our fellow humans and thus constantly tames our tendency to pursue our own mere self-interest.[6] If we wanted to make a bold comparison, we could say that Shaftesbury's positive anthropology paved the way for a positive treatment of recognition in great Britain just as La Rochefoucauld's negative anthropology had done for the negative discussion of recognition in France. Soon after Mandeville poured scorn on Shaftesbury's naïve optimism, the Scottish enlightenment philosopher Francis Hutcheson

---

[6] Anthony Ashley Cooper, Third Earl of Shaftesbury, "Sensus Communis, an essay on the freedom of wit and humour in a letter to a friend", in *Characteristics of Men, Manners, Opinions, Times*, ed. Lawrence Klein (Cambridge: Cambridge University Press, 1999), pp. 29–68.

would come to his defense, thereby founding the philosophical movement later known as Scottish moral philosophy. Instead of making mere anthropological claims, Hutcheson employed the nascent empiricism of his day to show that our reactions to others' behavior is generally determined by criteria of judgment which reveal our preference for beliefs and attitudes that are beneficial to the general well-being. From an assortment of facts about our everyday dealings, he believes he can infer a natural inclination for the well-being of fellow humans, which he in turn claims to be the foundation of all our moral principles.[7] This concept of a "moral sense", first raised by Shaftesbury and further developed by Hutcheson, laid the groundwork for what would develop in a few decades and with the help of further differentiations into what we could call a specifically British version of the idea of recognition, one that is diametrically opposed to the Hobbesian tradition, which C. B. Macpherson is somewhat justified in calling "possessive individualism".[8]

While working on his third volume of *A Treatise of Human Nature*, which deals with "morality",[9] David Hume was certainly aware of how much his theory owed to the

---

[7] Francis Hutcheson, *An Inquiry into the Original of our Ideas of Beauty and Virtue* (Carmel, IN: Liberty Fund, 2010). See also Wolfgang H. Schrader, *Ethik und Anthropologie in der englischen Aufklärung: Der Wandel der moral-sense-theorie von Shaftesbury bis Hume* (Hamburg: Meiner, 1984), esp. ch. 3.

[8] C. B. Macpherson, *The Political Theory of Possessive Individualism: Hobbes to Locke* (Oxford: Oxford University Press, 1962).

[9] David Hume, *A Treatise of Human Nature* (Oxford: Clarendon Press, 1888), Book 3: *Of Morals*.

writings of Hutcheson. Hume not only approaches the phenomenon of morality by empirically examining how we humans react and evaluate others' behavior, but he also agrees that such reactions primarily derive from natural sentiments rather than from rational knowledge. And yet, as soon as Hume begins to empirically substantiate the considerations that stand on these two pillars, he sees himself compelled to revise Hutcheson's assumptions; and these revisions ultimately carry him far beyond Hutcheson's own theory of morality.[10] Of Hume's many corrections and additions, two are of particular significance for our purposes as they lead us directly into the heart of Hume's conception of interpersonal recognition. The first of his improvements concerns Hutcheson's claim that we judge others' characteristics according to whether they are beneficial or harmful to the general well-being of the community. Hume agrees with this general claim, noting in addition that our reactions of approval or disapproval ultimately must be traced back to natural sentiments of pleasure or displeasure; however, he believes that Hutcheson has not sufficiently clarified the connection between such reactive sentiments and moral judgments. It remains unclear why we experience others' behavior, which we experience with pleasure or displeasure, as also being morally commendable or reprehensible. Hume believes that the explanation for such a connection between

---

[10] See Fate Norton, "Hume, Human Nature and the Foundation of Morality", pp. 155ff. See in particular Stephen Darwall, *The British Moralists and the Internal "Ought": 1640–1740* (Cambridge: Cambridge University Press, 1995), pp. 284–88.

feelings of pleasure or displeasure and moral judgments lies in a peculiar human disposition he terms "sympathy". This denotes our natural ability to understand others' mental states and experience them in our own minds.[11] In order to explain why "sympathy" is neither a mere passion nor a specific human need, but a kind of inevitable co-experience, Hume employs the famous image of two violin strings that set each other in motion simultaneously:

> As in strings equally wound up, the motion of one communicates itself to the rest; so all the affections readily pass from one person to another, and beget correspondent movements in every human creature. When I see the effects of passion in the voice and gesture of any person, my mind immediately passes from these effects to their causes, and forms such a lively idea of the passion, as is presently converted into the passion itself.[12]

This reference to "sympathy" gives an answer to the question of the internal connection between personality characteristics, positive and negative emotional reactions, and moral judgments by claiming that our shared experience of emotion with others enables us to judge whether another person experiences a given behavior as beneficial or harmful. According to Hume, we generally tend to morally approve or commend characteristics that manifest themselves in actions whose beneficial effects on others we can spontaneously co-experience due to our capacity for sympathy. Summarizing Hume's first correction of Hutcheson's conception, we could

[11] Hume, *Treatise*, pp. 576–8. [12] Ibid., p. 576.

say that an invisible bond of reciprocal co-experiencing moves us to react intuitively with positive feelings of approval to those human characteristics we feel are beneficial to the persons affected by them. Of course, it would be an exaggeration to claim that Hume had thereby already paved the way to a conception of interpersonal recognition. All we know at this point is that subjects have an almost natural capacity for emotional co-experiencing which enables them to understand and feel the well-being and suffering of others. But in order to arrive at a relationship we would be justified in calling "recognition", we still need to add the ascription of a certain amount of authority to the other – in the same way as Rousseau described the matter with regard to "amour propre", in which he declares the other to be a judge of the quality of our own characteristics. As long as the other is merely experienced as a subject whose emotions we can feel, we cannot yet speak of "recognition". Although such an "emotional co-vibration" (Ernst Tugendhat)[13] is a necessary precondition of all recognition, as this is what discloses the other as a subject in the first place,[14] a sense of normative dependence on the other is required before we can speak of genuine interpersonal recognition. Hume takes this step by making a further improvement on Hutcheson's concept of "moral sense", one which finally allows us to speak of the beginnings of a specifically British idea of recognition.

[13] Ernst Tugendhat, *Vorlesungen über Ethik* (Frankfurt: Suhrkamp, 1993), p. 308.

[14] See my own considerations in Axel Honneth, *Reification: A New Look at an Old Idea* (Oxford: Oxford University Press, 2008), ch. 3.

Only a few pages after claiming that "sympathy" represents the psychological basis of our concordance in the moral judgment of personal characteristics, Hume runs into a complication he feels might call into question his previous considerations.[15] He realizes that the sympathy underlying our approval or disapproval of others can be modified in a number of different ways depending on the degree of our social distance from those subjects whose behavior we observe. The closer and more familiar a person is to us, the stronger we will be able to sympathize with the positive or negative effects that person's actions have on his well-being. We must, therefore, have a tendency to be all the stricter in our judgment of character the closer we are to that person. Hume thus objects to his own argumentation:

> We sympathize more with persons contiguous to us, than with persons remote from us: With our acquaintance, than with strangers: With our countrymen, than with foreigners. But notwithstanding this variation of our sympathy we give the same approbation to the same moral qualities in China as in England. They appear equally virtuous, and recommend themselves equally to the esteem of a judicious spectator. The sympathy varies without a variation in our esteem. Our esteem, therefore, proceeds not from sympathy.[16]

In order to refute this potential objection, Hume now advances an argument that ultimately allows the outlines of an independent idea of interpersonal recognition to emerge. Hume begins by claiming that humans normally have both the

---

[15] Hume, *Treatise*, pp. 581ff.   [16] Ibid., p. 581.

cognitive capacity and the will to compensate for irregularities in their moral judgments of personal characteristics. As soon as we have an inkling that our judgments might be biased, Hume is convinced we will immediately make an effort to ensure that our judgments are more objective. He then attempts to discover the means by which we customarily neutralize possible biases, arguing that we necessarily allow ourselves to be taught by an ideal or "just" observer what an appropriate judgment would look like, regardless of time or place:

> It is impossible we could ever converse together on any reasonable terms, were each of us to consider characters and persons, only as they appear from his peculiar point of view. In order, therefore, to prevent those continual contradictions, and arrive at a more stable judgment of things, we fix on some steady and general points of view.[17]

Even if Hume does not mention the concept of an "ideal" spectator, the latter certainly stands in the background of his search for the procedure he believes we employ almost automatically to ensure that our moral judgments are as objective as possible. This notion of a neutral observer becomes much more explicit in his *Enquiry Concerning the Principles of Morals*,[18] which he published twelve years later and which he took to be "incomparably the best" of all his writings.[19] In this second book on moral theory, he speaks at many points

---

[17] Ibid., pp. 581f.
[18] David Hume, *Enquiry Concerning the Principles of Morals* (Oxford: Oxford University Press, 1998).
[19] David Hume, "My Own Life", in *The Letters of David Hume*, ed. John Y. T. Greig, 2 vols (Oxford: Oxford University Press, 1932), vol. 1, p. 3.

of the correcting role of a "spectator", which he describes either as a real person or as a fictitious figure that we internalize.[20] The basic thought remains the same: the notion of a judging gaze compels us to cleanse our judgments of impure preferences and give them an unbiased coherence. We therefore encounter, right in the middle of British empiricism, the same kind of external judge we saw in Rousseau's distinction between "amour propre" and "amour de soi". In the work of David Hume, however, this judge has the morally beneficial function of freeing our judgments from inconsistencies and biases.

Throughout his life Hume puzzled over the status of this "spectator" in the formation of our individual judgments. The only thing of which he is certain is that we almost instinctually examine our own moral evaluations in terms of whether such a neutral spectator could agree to them, yet Hume never fully clarifies just how we encounter this spectator – as a real community of other judging humans or as an internalized and imagined judge? Sometimes he suggests that we constantly attempt to correct our own particular standpoint by taking into account the perspective of concrete others; at other times he makes no mention of this correcting authority at all, and sometimes he even says that "reason requires such an impartial conduct"[21] – a claim which would contradict Hume's own internalism, according to which only our inner desires can move us to act morally.[22]

---

[20] Hume, *Enquiry.* [21] Hume, *Treatise*, p. 583.

[22] On this tension in Hume's theory of morality, see Herline Pauer-Studer, "Kommentar", in David Hume, *Über Moral*, rev. Herlinde Pauer-Studer (Frankfurt: Suhrkamp, 2007), pp. 213–373, here pp. 281f.

Therefore, if we exclude this last possibility, which incidentally displays a dubious similarity to Kant's rationality, we are left with the first two alternatives. Regardless of which of these interpretations we prefer, both contain different versions of the same reference to a necessary act of recognition on the part of others. Whether we grasp the "fair enquirer" as truly existing or as imagined spectators, in both cases we must accord to these representatives of an external subjectivity a measure of normative authority that is binding for our own actions and judgments. At the same time that Hume claims an impartial spectator to be indispensable for the formation of individual judgments, he also concedes that every subject grants other subjects the role of judge over its own intentions and preferences. Nobody decides alone what they should or should not do, rather other persons – whether real or imagined – are always already constitutively involved in the process by which every subject forms its beliefs and desires. An interpersonal relationship characterized by the fact that I grant another person the normative authority to judge my own behavior can certainly be understood as a kind of one-sided recognition. Because Hume further assumes, however, that we all encounter each other in this manner, we can even say that he gives an indication of an at least instinctual and reflex-like form of mutual recognition.

There are a number of other elements in Hume's theory of morality which support the claim that his considerations on the impartial formation of judgments represent an initial and cautious exploration of the sphere of interpersonal recognition. For instance, in his *Enquiry Concerning the Principles of Morals* he writes that the striving for "a name, a reputation in the world" causes us constantly to examine how our actions "appear in the eyes of those who approach and regard us".[23] If we read further, it becomes even more apparent that Hume's reference to our desire for social "reputation" aims at the motive for constantly examining our own judgments and actions in terms of whether they are worthy of social approval. A similar thought can also be found in the second part of his "treatise" dealing with "passions", in which he states that the "love of fame" can primarily be satisfied by constantly examining our actions in terms of others' expectations.[24] These passages all amount to the same thesis, and they cast a somewhat different light on what has been said thus far, for Hume now seems to claim that the habit of examining our moral thought and behavior from the perspective of an impartial spectator is primarily due to our desire to have a good reputation in the eyes of our peers. This presumption is entirely compatible with Hume's internalism, which states that our motive for examining our intentions from the perspective of a neutral spectator stems from our innermost desires. It is thus not just any imposed rule or reason which compels us to examine our opinions and intentions

---

[23] Hume, *Enquiry*, p. 76.

[24] Hume, *Treatise*, pp. 316–24. This chapter makes clear why Hume believes, contrary to Rousseau, that we retain mental control over which features we "truly" possess even if others show us great esteem: "The praises of others never give us much pleasure, unless they concur with our own opinion, and extol us for those qualities, in which we chiefly excel" (p. 322).

in terms of their impartial approvability, but our own "concern for our reputation".[25]

If we compare Hume's conclusion to Rousseau's account of "amour propre", we will find two almost diametrically opposed views of the function and functioning of interpersonal recognition. Whereas Rousseau sees the striving for social esteem as plunging humans into a maelstrom of epistemic self-doubt, Hume views this striving as compelling us to subject our intentions to the verdict of an impartial spectator, thus benefiting the general well-being. For Rousseau our dependence on "recognition" entails subjecting ourselves to the dictatorial authority of public opinion, while Hume sees us thereby granting the normative authority to co-determine the direction of our own behavior. In order to explain these major differences, we will have to reflect upon the different philosophical traditions that represent the theoretical horizon for their respective intellectual cultures. We saw that Rousseau grew up intellectually in the shadow of a skeptical image of human nature disseminated by the French moralists over the course of the sixteenth and seventeenth centuries in France. Hume, by contrast, picked up on the optimistic anthropology developed by Shaftesbury and Hutcheson in Great Britain. But in order to explain why Rousseau and Hume so willingly adopted the theoretical suggestions of their respective predecessors and sought to develop them in the same respective direction, we must turn to other, more profound continuities in the sociocultural climate of their respective homelands. I mentioned that

---

[25] Ibid., p. 501.

Rousseau's skeptical appraisal of social recognition likely derives from the historical experience of the Ancien Régime in which the nobility and the early bourgeoisie fought over royal privileges while employing all means of symbolic distinction. Even today this epoch of French history is regarded as a time in which politics was largely dictated by the struggle of the ruling classes for social distinction.[26] I mentioned in the same vein that Hume's positive image of a community based on recognition may be understood as an attempt to employ philosophical means to counter the processes of commercialization regarded as a significant challenge to social life in seventeenth-century Great Britain. The evidence of the eminent significance of this sense of danger in British intellectual culture is made apparent by the wide-ranging debates about the social role of "homo oeconomicus" reaching back to the Renaissance.[27]

All the evidence we could find in Hume's work to demonstrate the sociocultural roots of the specifically British view of recognition is put to shame by the theory of morality developed by his successor, Adam Smith. It is only in the latter's writings that the extremely positive connotation attached to interpersonal recognition in eighteenth-century Great Britain comes into full view – in the form of a philosophical reaction to what was generally regarded as a threat: the gradual commercialization of social mores. For many years, however, the close link between ethics and

---

[26] See Fanny Cosandey, *Le rang: Préséances et hierarchies dans la France d'Ancien Régime* (Paris: Gallimard, 2016).

[27] See again Volkmann, *Homo oeconomicus.*

economics in Smith's work would be ignored, because his works were divided into two irreconcilable parts. On the one hand, there is his book on "moral sentiments", a study in moral philosophy on the meaning of human benevolence; on the other hand, there is his *Wealth of Nations*, a study in economics focusing solely on the utility of human self-interest, without any internal connection having been recognized between these two doctrines published seventeen years apart. This unfortunate phase in the history of ideas would not end until the close of the nineteenth century. At this time in Germany the so-called "Adam Smith problem" was born, which refers to the anomalous gap that was said to exist between the economist and the moral philosopher.[28] In an important essay, the economist August Oncken proposed that we search for the bridge between Smith's two major works by focusing on the concept of "benevolence"; after all, this is how Smith justified his calls for restricting private egotism in the market.[29] This proposal fundamentally changed our view of the Scottish philosopher. Today, hardly any leading interpreter doubts the continuity in Smith's work, nor that we must interpret *The Wealth of Nations* from the perspective of his previous theory of moral sentiments.[30] I would like to

---

[28] On this debate see Keith Tribe, "'Das Adam Smith Problem' and the Origins of Modern Smith Scholarship", *History of European Ideas*, no. 4 (2008), pp. 514–25.

[29] August Oncken, "Das Adam Smith-Problem", *Zeitschrift für Sozialwissenschaft*, nos 1 (1898), pp. 25–33, 2 (1898), pp. 101–8, and 4 (1898), pp. 276–87.

[30] See e.g. Samuel Fleischacker, *Adam Smith's "Wealth of Nations": A Philosophical Companion* (Princeton: Princeton University Press,

take advantage of this new Smith reception by interpreting Adam Smith's theory of morality as a significantly improved and more consistent version of the theory of recognition we find in the work of David Hume. By doing so, I hope to be able to show the specifically British voice in the modern European discourse on human intersubjectivity.

The fact that the discussion of the consequences of our dependence on social recognition in Europe was in fact carried out across national borders can be seen in a small but interesting detail in Smith's work. At the beginning of the second part of his above-mentioned essay on the "Adam Smith problem", August Oncken remarks in passing that in earlier editions of Smith's *Theory of Moral Sentiments*, Smith intended his theory as a critique not only of Mandeville's *Fable of the Bees*, but also of La Rochefoucauld's *Maxims*. After exchanging several letters with a descendent of La Rochefoucauld, however, Smith decided to show his consideration for the latter's family by dropping his negative comments on the *Maxims*, such that his critique can no longer be found in current editions of the work. Whatever we might think of Smith's personal reasons for abandoning his critique, it does make perfectly clear that Adam Smith was entirely aware of being involved in a debate on self-referentiality and intersubjectivity taking place throughout Europe. On the one side, there were thinkers he labelled "materialists" due to their emphasis on human egotism, and to which he also added French thought on "amour propre"; and on the other side,

2004); Charles Griswold, *Adam Smith and the Virtues of Enlightenment* (Cambridge: Cambridge University Press, 1999).

there were primarily Scottish thinkers who like Smith himself assumed a natural human intersubjectivity grounded in our capacity for sympathy. In this sense, in a crucial passage of *Theory of Moral Sentiments,* Smith accuses his "materialist" opponents of misunderstanding the true relationship between humans:

> That whole account of human nature, however, which deduces all sentiments and affections from self-love, which has made so much noise in the world, but which, so far as I know, has never yet been fully and distinctly explained, seems to me to have arisen from some confused misapprehension of the system of sympathy.[31]

If we want to understand the highly original ideas Smith develops on interpersonal recognition, it is essential that we understand what he means by such a perspective on our "system of sympathy" cleansed of all misunderstandings.

I initially focused on those elements of David Hume's conception of morality I view as typical for how the idea of interpersonal recognition began to take hold in Great Britain starting at the close of the seventeenth century. In particular I addressed his claim that we attempt to correct irregularities and biases in our sympathy-based value judgments by taking up the perspective of an impartial spectator, thereby informing ourselves about judgment criteria that are more appropriate and as objective as possible. In this clever theoretical move of making our individual

---

[31] Adam Smith, *Theory of Moral Sentiments* (Cambridge: Cambridge University Press, 2002), pp. 374f.

judgments dependent on the judgment of an impartial spectator, I then found a reference to an original conception of interpersonal recognition. In effect, Hume concedes that we are willing to restrict our beliefs and intentions to a degree that could be seen as appropriate by a representative group of impartial spectators to whom we grant moral authority. To recognize somebody therefore means to grant another subject a particular normative status: the authority to inform us, through approval or disapproval, about the moral appropriateness of our own conduct. However, we also saw that Hume remains very vague on the issue of how such an impartial spectator comes to occupy this space in the spirit or psyche of the individual. Although he believes that our need for honor and reputation compels us to want to meet the normative expectations of our peers, this still does not explain why we should want our own conduct to be judged in an impartial and objective manner. After all, allowing our actions to be guided by the standpoint of our own moral group does not generally entail taking up the perspective of a "just", impartial judge. The "ideal" spectator that Hume has in mind seems to represent a case of *deus ex machina*, as he offers no precise empirical account of how this judge comes to have moral authority over us. This weak point in Hume's conception shows that he only went halfway in his attempt at an intersubjectivist refutation of the individualism prevalent in his day. Adam Smith would be the first to consummate the project initiated by Shaftesbury and Hutcheson, for he would show how we learn to make our moral conduct gradually dependent on ever more comprehensive forms of social recognition.

The point of departure for Smith's explorations into the field of morality is identical to that of Hutcheson and Hume, for Smith also poses the typical empiricist question about which criteria we apply in our everyday moral judgments of others' characteristics and social conduct. From Hume he adopts the premise that we are emotionally bound to others by a bond of sympathy enabling us to feel others' emotional reactions in ourselves. He then goes beyond Hume to warn us not to confuse our natural capacity for sympathy with the ability to experience others' emotions just as they do. Smith maintains that we cannot experience sympathy directly but must take a detour through our own experiences and employ our own imagination[32] in order to understand how others must feel: "In every passion of which the mind of man is susceptible, the emotions of the bystander always correspond to what, by bringing the case home to himself, he imagines should be the sentiments of the sufferer."[33] Therefore, the manner in which Smith defines our capacity for sympathy differs from that of his friend Hume; whereas the latter regards sympathy as a passive ability to be affected by the emotions of others, the former entertains the notion that we "projectively" feel such emotions by virtue of our imagination.[34] Moreover, Smith leaves no doubt that

---

[32] Ibid., pp. 11f. [33] Ibid., p. 13.

[34] This is the reason for the currently popular view that Hume possesses a "contagion account" of sympathy in contrast to Smith's "projection account". See Dennis C. Rasmussen, *The Infidel and the Professor: David Hume, Adam Smith, and the Friendship that Shaped Modern Thought* (Princeton: Princeton University Press, 2017), ch 5, esp. p. 92; Samuel Fleischacker, "Sympathy in Hume and Smith: A Contrast,

sympathy cannot mean actually feeling the "misery" or the "suffering" of the sufferer; this is only true in the case of "compassion" or "pity". Sympathy, by contrast, must be understood in a broader sense as the capacity to feel "any passion" of others.[35]

After making these preliminary conceptual clarifications, Smith then turns to the issue at the center of his attempt to found a theory of morality. He inquires into the moral attitudes and virtues which, given our natural capacity for sympathy, should count as universally valid, i.e. desirable to all subjects from the perspective of all subjects.[36] His argumentation in *Theory of Moral Sentiments* is far too convoluted and complex to be able to recapitulate it here fully; I will once again restrict my analysis, as in the case of Hume's concept of morality, to the core elements of Smith's idea of interpersonal recognition. His first step consists in the empirical observation that our natural tendency to sympathize with others corresponds to others' desire for our sympathy. Thus he writes at the beginning of the second chapter in the very first part of the book that "nothing pleases us more than to observe in other men a fellow-feeling with all the emotions of our own breast; nor are we ever so much shocked as by the appearance of the contrary."[37] He goes on to cite dozens of examples meant to

Critique, and Reconstruction", in Christel Fricke and Dagfinn Føllesdal, *Intersubjectivity and Objectivity in Adam Smith and Edmund Husserl: A Collection of Essays* (Frankfurt: Ontos, 2012), pp. 273–311.

[35] Smith, *Theory of Moral Sentiments*, p. 13.

[36] On this program see the reconstruction by Ernst Tugendhat in *Vorlesungen über Ethik*, pp. 282–309.

[37] Smith, *Theory of Moral Sentiments*, p. 17.

prove that regardless of how close or far we might be to others in our everyday lives, we always feel a great deal of pleasure whenever we find ourselves in emotional harmony with others. By contrast, when friends do not take pleasure in our joy over a fortunate occurrence, we are just as astonished or displeased as we would be if someone did not grieve with us in the face of a personal tragedy.[38] Smith's intention here is to prove just how much the need for bonds of emotional harmony with others is part of our human nature.

Of course, Smith is also aware that the mere expectation of such reciprocity in our emotional experience is not enough to reveal the principles that should dictate our dealings with others. In order to get a bit closer to the core of all morality, therefore, Smith goes on to address a number of complications that arise in the process of emotional harmonization, thereby hoping to attain a more precise idea of how this process works. His approach is similar to that of Hume, who also takes a detour through the irregularities of our moral evaluations in order to explore their true nature; Smith's elaborations, however, are far more extensive, enabling him to arrive at more differentiated results. He begins with what at first might seem to be a surprising observation, which is that we sympathize with others' suffering even if they show no signs of pain. Conversely, we will not be able to feel another person's pain if we regard the cause of that as being negligible or insignificant.[39] After adding further such examples, Smith becomes convinced that we do not merely feel sympathy because another person shows certain emotions through

[38] Ibid., pp. 17–20. [39] Ibid., p. 15.

facial expressions or gestures. Instead, by automatically employing our imagination we judge others' perceptible emotions in terms of whether they are in fact appropriate or inappropriate. The concept Smith employs in order to explain this fact is that of "propriety" or "suitability",[40] which means that our sympathy is always naturally guided by a normative criterion for determining whether a perceptible emotion is "proper" or suitable to the situation that causes it. Smith is clever enough to realize, however, that even this more profound analysis of our emotional "fellow-feeling" does not get us very far. Although we now know that we inevitably employ implicit normative criteria in judging the situational appropriateness of others' behavior, the origin of these criteria remains entirely unclear.

In order to bridge this explanatory gap, Smith takes a third step in his argumentation – one which consists of several levels and basically stretches over the entire book. He begins by pointing out that we generally judge the appropriateness, "propriety" or "suitability" of our own emotional reactions in terms of whether a given spectator of the same situation would agree with them. At first this merely means that by placing ourselves in the position of an external observer, we learn how we should react in an emotionally appropriate way to something that has happened to another person. According to Smith, however, the converse also applies to those who have been affected by a certain event. They, too, must ask themselves from the perspective of an external observer which emotional reaction is appropriate.[41]

---

[40] Ibid., p. 20. [41] Ibid., p. 123.

In this scenario, therefore, we are dealing with a kind of reciprocity that consists in a desire not only for shared emotions, but also for the approval of an external observer. Both subjects – the one who emotionally evaluates a situation and the one who is emotionally affected by that situation – want their reaction to find the approval not only of their partners in interaction, but also of an external observer. Perhaps we could also say that both subjects strive to regulate their harmonization from the perspective of a neutral spectator.

Smith must add two further elements to this model of emotional reciprocity in order to derive the ethical virtues he regards as universally justifiable in his naturalist ethic. First, he needs to clarify further the nature of the impartial spectator from whom both participants hope to receive approval for their mutually related emotional reactions. According to Smith, this spectator must become increasingly abstract in the course of mutual harmonization, as both participants will be compelled to draw upon additional voices of further impartial spectators in normatively assessing their own emotional conduct.[42] Moreover, if we follow the different stages of Smith's account, the process of generalizing this approving or disapproving other continues until this "all-seeing"[43] "Judge of the world"[44] coincides with "reason"[45] – a problematic reference given Smith's empiricism, but nevertheless a wonderful indication

---

[42] On this gradual expansion of "circles of sympathy" see Fonna Forman-Barzilai, *Adam Smith and the Circles of Sympathy: Cosmopolitanism and Moral Theory* (Cambridge: Cambridge University Press, 2010), ch. 5.

[43] Smith, *Theory of Moral Sentiments*, p. 153. [44] Ibid. [45] Ibid., p. 377.

of empiricism's significance for Kant.[46] Smith never leaves any doubt that we should imagine this generalized spectator as the inner voice of our conscience rather than as an external judge. At one point he writes, in another astounding anticipation of Kant, that every person carries a "representative" of this "impartial spectator" in the form of a "man within the breast".[47]

Although this explanation makes it unmistakably clear that we are to conceive of such emotional self-examination as the internalization of a gradually generalized other ultimately comprising the voices of all our fellow humans, a second question still remains unanswered, as it remains entirely unclear why we should be motivated to submit to such an examination of our emotional conduct. Whenever Smith addresses this problem in passing, he seems merely to repeat Hume's solution, which is that this motivation derives from our hope to achieve fame and social reputation.[48] However, once Smith addresses this issue directly, a much more complex conception becomes immediately apparent. For instance, in the second chapter of Part III,[49] he writes that we normatively examine our own emotional conduct not primarily to receive praise or affection, but to prove ourselves "praise-worthy". Therefore, we are generally not content to receive mere praise or basic affection; rather, we also always seek to know whether we are in

---

[46] See the contributions in Christel Fricke and Hans-Peter Schütt, eds, *Adam Smith als Moralphilosoph* (Berlin and New York: Campus, 2005). See also Samuel Fleischacker, "Philosophy and Moral Practice: Kant and Adam Smith", *Kant-Studien*, 3 (1991), pp. 249–69.

[47] Smith, *Theory of Moral Sentiments*, p. 178.   [48] See e.g. Ibid., pp. 60f.

[49] Ibid., pp. 128ff.

fact worthy of such praise or affection. Following Smith's oft-repeated formulation, we must conceive of the motive to normatively examine our own conduct as itself being "moral"; his summary of this point makes it sound as if he is seeking to make our happiness and contentment contingent on our constantly proving the praiseworthiness of our emotional conduct:

> The jurisdiction of the man within (impartial spectator) is founded altogether in the desire of praise-worthiness, and in the aversion to blame-worthiness; in the desire of possessing those qualities, and performing those actions, which we love and admire in other people; and in the dread of possessing those qualities, and performing those actions, which we hate and despise in other people.[50]

To elucidate the far-reaching implications of Smith's groundbreaking considerations would take us too far afield, for Smith claims that we should be willing to model our interpersonal emotions on the internalized verdict of a generalized other because we naturally seek "justified approval" (Tugendhat).[51] Depending on our philosophical stance, we can view this claim as a bold anticipation of Kant or as a regression behind the methodological premises of empiricism. We could also ask whether the trench Smith digs between our need for social praise and our interest in justified approval is so deep as to prevent any plausible mediation between these two desires. Occasionally it seems as if Smith already speaks of two human "natures", an "empirical"

---

[50] Ibid., p. 150. [51] Tugendhat, *Vorlesungen über Ethik*, p. 311.

and an "intelligible" nature.⁵² Leaving aside these questions and concerns, the passage does at least give us a clear sense of the idea of social recognition contained in Smith's theory of morality.

It is clear that recognition must entail a greater amount of normative concern and moral willingness than in the work of David Hume. Whereas Hume's theory of morality assumed that our egocentric interest in social reputation and status make us willing to grant normative authority to an unbiased spectator, Smith cannot and will not accept the premise of such a self-interested subject. He believes that the emotional bond of sympathy is anchored far too deep in the individual's personality for humans to be conceived of as initially isolated individuals who then come together by virtue of their mutual obedience to an impartial judge. For Smith, therefore, intersubjective recognition fundamentally requires that we regard all other individuals as beings to whom we wish to be joined through both our emotions and our experiences. Yet this elementary, natural form of recognition is, according to Smith, not sufficient to guarantee such "emotional communication" [*affektives Kommunizieren*]⁵³ between all human beings. On the basis of our individual preferences, cultural habits and personal biases, we are not automatically capable of sympathizing with others in the appropriate way. Smith therefore sees the need for a second

---

⁵² See e.g. the sentences before the cited passage, in which Smith speaks of the "two persons" in one and the same person: Smith, *Theory of Moral Sentiments*, p. 150.
⁵³ I owe the term "affektives Kommunizieren" to Ernst Tugendhat. See Tugendhat, *Vorlesungen über die Ethik*, p. 295.

stage of recognition, one which works to bring together the emotions and sentiments of isolated subjects. This new form of recognition consists in internalizing as many perspectives as possible in order to produce the voice of an impartial and knowledgeable judge to whom we grant the authority to harmonize our emotions with those of others by means of approval and disapproval. Whereas the first, emotional form of recognition is directly related to others, whom we assume to have the same need for communicative sympathy, the second form of recognition depends on a generalized other, and is thus indirect and aimed at others. In the latter case we pay recognition primarily to an idealized community of all members of society – a community which we internalize and equip with the moral authority to judge the appropriateness of our emotions and thus form the character of our individual self. Whether Smith was in fact right to regard this second form of recognition as a part of our first nature is a question that I will leave unanswered for the time being.[54]

However, nothing I have said up to this point about Smith's idea of recognition justifies the claim that he sought, like Hume, to ward off the egocentricity of his fellow countrymen – an attitude that became more and more rampant as the capitalist market spread. When it comes to David Hume, this claim might still sound somewhat plausible, as there is enough evidence that he had significant doubts about the idea that the common good could be served merely by means of the clever coordination of egocentric interests. Although Hume was highly interested in the new discipline of political economy

---

[54] See on this issue Smith, *Theory of Moral Sentiments*, pp. 227ff.

and even attempted to develop his own such theory,[55] he remained skeptical throughout his life about the claim that the fewer the moral restrictions, the better the market will function. As Mikko Tolonen has shown wonderfully in a recent study,[56] Hume defended the idea against Mandeville that if the market is to fulfill its tasks, it will require its own "political sociability", i.e. politically supported rules of conduct. The matter becomes more complicated once we turn to Adam Smith, for it is not so clear that his philosophical work sought primarily to oppose the capitalist market and its compulsion to pursue our own self-interest. Such an assumption conflicts at any rate with the traditional idea, which remains widespread even today, that the Scottish philosopher was primarily interested in justifying the free market. This interpretation thus exclusively cites Smith's *Wealth of Nations* to the utter exclusion of all of his contributions to moral philosophy in order to propagate the view that Smith was so convinced of the social utility of individual self-interest that he argued for a market that would be as unrestricted as possible.[57] I have already pointed out the absurdity of this interpretation of Smith's work in connection with the so-called "Adam Smith problem"; today we can say with some

---

[55] David Hume, "Of Commerce", in *David Hume's Writings on Economics* (New York: Transaction, 2007), pp. 3–18.

[56] Mikko Tolonen, *Mandeville and Hume: Anatomists of Civil Society* (Oxford: Oxford University Press, 2013), ch. 4.

[57] For an overview, see Emma Rotschild and Amartya Sen, "Adam Smith's Economics", in Knud Haakonssen, ed., *The Cambridge Companion to Adam Smith* (Cambridge: Cambridge University Press, 2006), pp. 319–65.

certainty that the further the interpretation of Smith's work progresses, the more the opposite view seems to prevail, which is that Smith's economic theory must be viewed in terms of his moral philosophy and thus cannot count as a straightforward defense of the free market.

As a result of this change of perspective, Smith's *Wealth of Nations* is for the most part no longer viewed as the prevalent ideology of "laissez faire". If we follow the interpretation offered by Samuel Fleischacker, for instance, Smith sought to show that the only justifiable elements of the capitalist market are those which could meet with the approval of an impartial and knowledgeable judge. Fleischacker thus also claims that Smith felt that any element of the capitalist system contradicting this procedural criterion should be criticized and perhaps even abolished.[58] If we read *Wealth of Nations* in this light, we will immediately notice the many elements of the text that seem to have the sole function of blocking the advance of economic self-interest on the market. Smith warns, for instance, of the destructive consequences of the unrestricted exploitation of factory workers' labor power for both the body and the mind.[59] He also suggests that we always keep in mind the ultimate goal of freeing wageworkers from servility and

[58] Fleischacker, *Adam Smith's 'Wealth of Nations'*, esp. pp. 48–57; see also the similar interpretations in Spencer J. Pack, *Capitalism as a Moral System: Adam Smith's Critique of the Free Market Economy* (Aldershot: Elgar, 1991), as well as Griswold, *Adam Smith and the Virtues of Enlightenment*.

[59] Adam Smith, *Wealth of Nations*, Book V (London: Penguin, 1989), pp. 368–9.

personal dependence.[60] And finally, he continually seeks to evaluate economic rules and regulations from the perspective of all those affected.[61] Certainly, none of these restrictions and suggestions necessarily proved to be the most effective means of restricting the capitalist market, but they do make very clear that Smith was anything but a fervent proponent of the advantages of economic self-interest. He did not intend the recognition we give to others by obeying the voice of our inner judge to end at the gates of this new economic system; on the contrary, he sought to anchor this voice in the market by means of procedural regulations and moral considerations.[62] Even if he might not have gone far enough in this direction and was certainly hesitant to consider state intervention in the market, his main purpose in *The Wealth of Nations* was to find adequate tools for restricting egocentric behavior in the economic sphere. Therefore, we might be justified after all in assuming that his philosophical aim was to counter the spread of capitalistic convictions by formulating relations of recognition that always already join us to each other, and that this aim is indeed pervasive throughout Smith's work. Like Hume, though with stronger intersubjective tendencies, Smith was convinced that we have a natural willingness to be educated by the praise and criticism of the generalized other of the community of all humans to behave in a way that promotes the common good.

[60] Ibid., pp. 167–90, 458–62.
[61] See again Fleischacker, *Adam Smith's "Wealth of Nations"*, pp. 49ff.
[62] Pack, *Capitalism as a Moral System*.

If we let eighty years pass and turn to the work of John Stuart Mill, it will immediately become clear that this specific idea about the value of intersubjective recognition did not remain an isolated appearance within Great Britain, a mere intellectual offshoot of Scottish moral philosophy. At first sight, Mill appears to be anything but an intersubjectivist thinker, as he is deeply convinced that everyone is responsible for their own happiness. Mill believed in the moral power of praise and blame, which, like Smith and Hume, he traced back to humans' need for social recognition. However, as decisive as this thought might have been for Mill's liberal agenda, it does not appear until very late in his theoretical argumentation, much later than in the work of both our Scottish philosophers. As we have seen, Hume regarded our striving for social reputation as compelling us to cleanse our value judgments of any social bias and to strive to make judgments that are cognitively coherent; Smith viewed our need to live in harmony with others as driving us to behave in a way that could be considered praiseworthy in the eyes of an impartial judge. For Mill, however, the role of a "generalized other" in our system of motivations was not of primary importance. Although he dedicated the third chapter of *Utilitarianism*, wholly in the spirit of Adam Smith, to the question of the degree to which humans possess "social feelings",[63] the relation of recognition interested him primarily in a sociopolitical sense.

---

[63] John Stuart Mill, *Utilitarianism* (Indianapolis: Hackett, 2001). See the passage which strongly resembles Smith: "The deeply rooted conception which every individual even now has of himself as a social being tends to make him feel it one of his natural wants that there should be harmony between his feelings and aims and those of his fellow creatures" (p. 34).

Mill's liberal polemic *On Liberty* is the primary place to find his considerations on this matter. The intellectual focus of this book is obviously the sociopolitical demand that all individuals be enabled to realize the characteristics and talents granted to them by nature without disruption or compulsion.[64] Mill encountered this ethical cornerstone of his liberal views after reading the writings of English and German Romanticism, finding there an entirely new conception of the uniqueness of human individuality. He became convinced that each individual possesses an individual core of unique capacities and desires that they attempt to develop over the course of their lives, similar to an organic process.[65] On the basis of this ideal Mill held that the primary task of liberal society was to ensure all the legal, economic and cultural conditions needed to enable individuals to realize their unique talents with as few restrictions as possible. In his work *On Liberty*, published in 1859, he summarizes for the first time his views on the makeup of social institutions. They should ensure basic freedoms of opinion, thought and discussion, restricting them only in rare exceptions;[66] they should ensure a sufficient amount of cultural diversity;[67] and finally, they should provide educational methods that teach children the entire spectrum of

[64] John Stuart Mill, *On Liberty* (Indianapolis: Hackett, 1978), ch. III.

[65] John Stuart Mill, *Autobiography* (London: Penguin, 1990). Mill develops this thought in *On Liberty*, ch. II. See also John Skorupski, *Why Read Mill Today* (London: Routledge, 2006), pp. 24–31.

[66] Mill, *On Liberty*, ch. II; see again Skorupski, *Why Read Mill Today*, pp. 41–51.

[67] Mill, *On Liberty*, ch. III.

different ways of living and thinking.[68] Moreover, if we look at his study *Chapters on Socialism*, which would remain uncompleted and was first published posthumously by Helen Taylor in 1879,[69] at the end of his life Mill seems to have been convinced that in addition to this set of basic liberties and institutions, the state is also obligated to initiate the exploration of new economic forms more beneficial to workers.

Of course, this catalog of sociopolitical demands raises a number of questions, since Mill provides no methodological framework – though this hardly need concern us here. To begin with, we would have to clarify whether Mill sought to justify his reform proposals in a utilitarian or a perfectionist manner, that is, whether his conception of the good life consisted in the sum of the greatest good for all or as the institutional epitome of a conception of the good life without any utilitarian aims. This raises a meta-ethical question first posed by Isaiah Berlin in order to cast doubt on the notion that Mill should be considered a utilitarian,[70] although this is irrelevant for our interest in determining the role of the concept of recognition in Mill's work. Of far greater relevance

---

[68] Ibid., pp. 108–9.

[69] John Stuart Mill, *Principles of Political Economy and Chapters on Socialism* (Oxford: Oxford University Press, 2008). On Mill's complex relationship with socialism, see C. L. Ten, "Democracy, Socialism, and the Working Classes", in John Skorupski, ed., *The Cambridge Companion to Mill* (Cambridge: Cambridge University Press, 1988), pp. 372–95.

[70] Isaiah Berlin, "John Stuart Mill and the Ends of Life", in *Four Essays on Liberty* (Oxford: Oxford University Press, 1969), pp. 173–206.

is the often-discussed question of the means of social control Mill envisioned for dealing with collisions between the institutionally supported process of individual self-realization and the self-realization of others. Mill felt that such conflicts should be resolved by means of the so-called "harm principle", which stipulates that a person's or group's opinions or lifestyle can be justifiably suppressed if they restrict or harm others' parallel attempts at self-realization.[71] Mill went to great efforts to pinpoint the normative threshold for such harm. In *Utilitarianism*, he writes that due to the moral progress of society, each individual possesses inviolable "moral rights";[72] the same rights reappear in *On Liberty*, though here Mill is primarily concerned with extending this limit so as to grant individuals as much freedom to experiment as possible, even if this entails the freedom to do harm to themselves.[73] In decisive passages in both of these books, Mill remarks that the most appropriate means of preventing or arbitrating such conflicts consists in motivating subjects, through moral praise and blame, to respect the interests of their peers. Mill is convinced that when it comes to preventing collisions between diverse forms of individual self-realization, public approval or disapproval is much more effective than the threat of legal punishment. Whenever he proposes this social instrument, of course, he also raises the concern of

[71] Mill formulates this principle in chapter IV of *On Liberty*. On the difficulties involved in implementing this principle, see John Skorupski, *John Stuart Mill* (London: Routledge, 1989), pp. 340–3.

[72] Mill, *Utilitarianism*, ch. V. See also Skorupski, *Why Read Mill Today*, pp. 34–8.

[73] Mill, *On Liberty*, ch. IV.

a "tyranny of the majority", of the domination of a "moral police"[74] that might suppress any potential for innovation in our way of life. In this case public approval or disapproval would not serve to stimulate our moral self-control, but would merely suppress any creative impulses for social reinvention. Despite these concerns, however, Mill remained convinced that cautious, liberal public praise and blame represent, at least for the time being, society's best means for avoiding collisions between conflicting ways of life.

Mill appears to locate the reason for the effectiveness of moral disapproval in a basic feature of human nature he discusses at various points in his writings. At this specific point in his sociopolitical considerations, we finally encounter Mill's own idea of recognition. He holds that we allow public disapproval to move us to show moral consideration for others because of our deep-seated need for social esteem; our desire to be respected members of society thus makes public disapproval an effective motivational force. The experience of being reprimanded in front of our fellow citizens will eventually cause us to fear being excluded from the community, compelling us to agree to respect society's norms. For Mill, therefore, the social bond that holds together a community is woven from the fabric of mutual recognition; he thus writes in *Utilitarianism* that "the fear of displeasure from our fellow creatures" is what "inclines" us to respect the will of the community "independently of selfish consequences".[75]

---

[74] The term "moral police" is found in *On Liberty*, pp. 82, 86.
[75] Mill, *Utilitarianism*, p. 28.

Therefore, essentially the same idea of recognition we encountered in the work of David Hume and Adam Smith reappears in John Stuart Mill's sociopolitical considerations. Although this utilitarian thinker – if indeed he is one – abstains entirely from the notion of an impartial spectator or inner judge, he does believe like both of his Scottish predecessors that we are willing, for the sake of being esteemed by the community, to subject our motives and intentions to an inner authority that morally aligns them with those of our peers. Even if none of these three philosophers ever explicitly employed the term "recognition", they do have a positive view of that to which "recognition" refers. For Mill, just as for Hume and Smith, our dependence on others' judgment primarily means that we are compelled to examine our own conduct in terms of its compatibility with the normative expectations of the – idealized or real – community of our peers.[76]

We can only speculate about the cause of this harmony with regard to the idea of recognition in Great Britain. At the very start of my discussion of the case of Great Britain, I presumed that this might be due to the fact that capitalist mentalities spread more rapidly there than in the rest of Europe. I claimed that in order to counter these cultural tendencies with philosophical means, seventeenth- and eighteenth-century British thinkers felt compelled to emphasize humans' social nature in contrast to Hobbes'

---

[76] Peter Stemmer bases his ontological justification of "normativity" not on the German but on this British concept of recognition: *Normativität: Eine ontologische Untersuchung* (Berlin: de Gruyter, 2008), esp. §8.

"possessive individualism".[77] The example of John Stuart Mill seems to me to confirm this presumption for the nineteenth century as well, as Mill also perceived the increase of egotism, greed and social recklessness as the defining features of British life. He too saw a need to combat this mentality by means of a theory that emphasizes concern for the community. The reason for this thinker's impulse to engage in a sympathetic discussion of early socialism in his old age is obviously due to this same motive; he repeatedly mentions the dangerously weak "sentiment of the community" and the growing "greed of rapid gain",[78] which needs to be combated by institutional means with the help of socialist proponents.

Now it might seem as if we could complete this sketch of the specifically British understanding of recognition by casting a brief glance at late nineteenth-century Neo-Hegelianism, which broke the dominance of Mill in British philosophy.[79] At first sight, this philosophical and social movement seems to have drawn on German Idealism in order to build upon the intersubjectivism already found in the work of Hume, Smith and even Mill. The movement picked up on the works of Kant and Hegel, whose concept of positive freedom provided a clear demonstration of individuals' dependence on a supportive society – a stark contrast to the individualism prevalent in Great Britain at the time. Thomas Hill Green

---

[77] Macpherson, *Possessive Individualism*.

[78] Mill, *Principles of Political Economy and Chapters on Socialism*, p. 406.

[79] See Peter P. Nicholson, *The Political Philosophy of the British Idealists* (Cambridge: Cambridge University Press, 1990).

and Francis Herbert Bradley sought to show that individuals become moral persons by learning to adopt the rules of the social community in which they live and behave in accordance with them.[80] This meant for both philosophers that society is obligated to provide the social conditions required for learning and adopting the rules of the community.[81] Therefore, the proponents of this new philosophical movement assumed that the process of individual self-realization coincides with the ethical perfecting of society; they drew the political conclusion that welfare-state reforms are needed to integrate the working class into the democratic constitutional state.[82] If we also take into consideration just how vehemently this movement rebelled against the excesses of Manchester capitalism, then it seems clear that everything I have said about the idea of recognition in the work of Hume, Smith and Mill is even more true of British Neo-Hegelianism. Yet, there is one serious problem that prevents me from completing my reconstruction in this manner. The theoretical efforts of Green, Bradley and Bosanquet are so clearly imported from German Idealism that they bear hardly any trace of a specifically British style of thinking.[83] Neo-Hegelianism does not represent a further

---

[80] Thomas H. Green, *Prolegomena to Ethics*, ed. D. O. Brink (Oxford: Oxford University Press, 2003); Francis H. Bradley, *Ethical Studies* (Oxford: Oxford University Press, 1876).

[81] See e.g. Thomas H. Green, *Lectures on the Principles of Political Obligation* (London: Longmans, 1924), pp. 121–41.

[82] Melvin Richter, *The Politics of Conscience: T. H. Green and His Age* (London: Weidenfeld & Nicolson, 1964).

[83] Very illumination on this connection is the introduction by D. O. Brink in Green, *Prolegomena to Ethics*, pp. xiii–cx.

development of the tradition of Scottish moral philosophy in terms of the social nature of human beings; rather, it discloses the nature of human intersubjectivity against the conceptual horizon of a tradition which draws its major impulses from its opposition to intellectual currents such as English empiricism.[84] The idea of recognition found in British Neo-Hegelianism, therefore, is very distinct from the idea I have described as being typical of philosophical discourse in Great Britain at the onset of modernity. What Hume, Smith and their followers regard as an empirical matter, i.e. the motivating moral force of our dependence on others' approval or esteem, British Neo-Hegelians take to be a constitutive condition of our moral subjectivity. The true depth of this chasm will not become apparent until we have investigated the distinctiveness of the concept of recognition in German thought. Therefore, I will now turn to this task of reconstructing the origin and development of the idea of recognition in Germany at the onset of modernity.

[84] See John Skorupski, *English-Language Philosophy 1750–1945* (Oxford: Oxford University Press, 1993), ch. 3.

4

From Kant to Hegel
Recognition and Self-Determination

We have now seen two very different conceptions of our dependence on the recognition of others emerging and consolidating at the onset of modernity. Whereas French thinkers of the time were quick to view this dependence as a threat, fearing that the social ascription of personal characteristics might cause us to lose sight of our own nature, British thinkers since the time of the Enlightenment regarded this dependence as something positive and socially valuable. For all the differences between them, Hume, Smith and Mill nevertheless shared the view that the awareness of our dependence on others' esteem compels us to judge our own actions morally, which contributes to the well-being of society as a whole. Depending on the philosophical culture, therefore, "recognition" takes on strikingly different meanings. In the French context, it is primarily viewed from the perspective of the (either concrete or general) other and means conceding or according personal characteristics; in the British context, the perspective is that of the recognizing subject and means conceding to other individuals or the social community as a whole the normative authority to judge the morality of our own conduct. In these two contexts, recognition is rarely conceived of as an occurrence of simultaneous mutuality between two equal subjects. In my view, this conception only arises in the German context, where the origin of the term also represented the origin of a whole theory of recognition.

The sociocultural conditions underlying this philosophical development in early modern Germany were very different from those in France or Great Britain. In France during the time of the Ancien Régime and under the rule of a highly centralized, absolutist monarchy, the struggle among the dominant factions of the nobility and the early bourgeoisie over privileges granted by the king – a struggle carried out with every imaginable means of social distinction – led to major changes in the social structures. My presumption, therefore, was that for a long period of time the key issue of philosophical discourse in France was the dubious consequences of this struggle over fame and honor for those compelled to engage in it. In Great Britain, by contrast, the major changes of the time were perceived less in terms of social conflict than in terms of a danger to morally binding forms of life. As I have attempted to show, the key issue of social-philosophical thought in Great Britain was the question of whether we are naturally capable of the solidarity needed to resist the rise of capitalist mentalities such as egotism and greed. Such sociocultural particularities would become strikingly apparent in the conceptions of intersubjective relations that began to circulate in both these countries. In France, the concept of "amour propre" represented a pejorative vehicle for the idea of recognition, while in Great Britain the positively connoted idea of "sympathy" played the same role. Yet, neither of these can be considered the decisive challenge for social-philosophical thought in the German Reich at the onset of modernity. This highly fragmented political mosaic of numerous principalities along with a small number of "free" cities lacked any real internal political bonds; it was not centralistic enough to enable something like a struggle of social elites over power and privilege. And the country was not sufficiently developed economically to permit more than a vague sense of the rise of capitalist mentalities. Owing to the enduring influence of feudal power structures, the bourgeoisie outside the free cities possessed no political power, though it did enjoy a very positive social reputation in contrast to other European countries at the time, being indispensable for the tasks of administration, education and cultural life.[1] We are therefore entirely justified in asking whether the highly fragmented political life and backwardness of Germany in the seventeenth and eighteenth centuries could have at all permitted something like a single social challenge for German thinkers. We might presume that in many places the feudal order was still far too intact for the questionable nature of the social structure of recognition to become a real issue. Yet this was in fact not the case; even in politically fragmented Germany we find a social-philosophical problem no politically minded contemporary could ignore. This was due to the typical disjuncture between the political insignificance of the bourgeoisie and its enormously important cultural role. Contrary to the situation in France, the most significant intellectuals, philosophers and artists in the German Reich

---

[1] Seigel, *Modernity and Bourgeois Life*, pp. 114ff. On the particular role of the bourgeoisie in fragmented Germany, see Helmuth Plessner, *Die verspätete Nation: Über die politische Verführbarkeit bürgerlichen Geistes* (Frankfurt: Suhrkamp, 1974), chs 4–6.

stemmed not from the nobility, but almost exclusively from the middle and lower bourgeoisie. As the son[2] of a craftsman, priest, teacher or professor, a person employed at the university, in the royal court or in the households of the nobility might have enjoyed the highest cultural reputation, but had no political influence of any kind – perhaps with the exception of Leibniz and Goethe, both sons of the bourgeoisie, whose diplomatic skills enabled them to gain a measure of influence on their superiors. As a consequence, the question that would soon arise in the German Reich with regard to social structures of interaction concerned the conditions for the emancipation of the bourgeoisie, the achievement of political equality and rights to co-determination. It can be of no surprise, therefore, that in early modern Germany the idea of recognition primarily had the function of supporting the notion of the equality of all citizens and manifested itself in a form that, philosophically speaking, was highly peculiar.

We might be tempted to search for the first traces of such an idea of recognition in the work of the two greatest German intellectuals of the seventeenth century: Samuel Pufendorf and Gottfried Wilhelm Leibniz. After all, Pufendorf's assumption that humans are naturally social and equal laid the groundwork for the modern idea of natural law,[3] and Leibniz was no less convinced of our natural

---

[2] The authors we will be discussing here are, typically for the time, exclusively male.

[3] On the role of Pufendorf in preparing the ground for the modern idea of individual self-determination, see Jerome B. Schneewind, *The Invention of Autonomy: A History of Modern Moral Philosophy* (Cambridge: Cambridge University Press, 1988), ch. 7.

penchant for sociality, although he based a concept of social order on this assumption that might seem quite utilitarian to us today.[4] But to want to find such predecessors would mean underestimating the utter novelty of the intellectual conditions surrounding the emergence of the idea of recognition in the second half of the eighteenth century in Germany. Over the three generations passing between the works of Leibniz and the height of German Idealism, a revolution took place in German thinking, one which would make all previous philosophical thought appear positively obsolete. Kant had introduced a kind of systematic thinking which sought to capture the entirety of the world in categories of practical reason; within this systematic framework of rational Idealism, the idea of recognition would unfold. Kant would pioneer the concept, its first true representative would be Johann Gottlieb Fichte, and it would become fully developed in the work of Georg Wilhelm Friedrich Hegel.

While the idea of recognition had its breakthrough in France with the concept of "amour propre" and in Great Britain with the concept of "sympathy", in Germany it was the term "respect" [*Achtung*]. For Kant, this term fulfilled a very specific task in his moral philosophy, which can only be understood by taking the entirety of his critique of reason into consideration. In his *Critique of Pure Reason* (1781), the Königsberg philosopher first sought to prove that our theoretical knowledge is the product of a synthesis between fixed,

---

4 Gottfried Wilhelm Leibniz, "Über die öffentliche Glückseligkeit", in *Politische Schriften II*, ed. H. H. Holz (Frankfurt and Vienna: EVA, 1967), pp. 134f.

transcendental categories and sense impressions. To para-phrase Kant, we can only understand those parts of reality given to the spontaneous activity of our mind with the help of the latter's own, invariable concepts. By making such a groundbreaking claim, Kant not only sought to put the epistemological claims of British empiricism in their place, but also the entirety of traditional metaphysics. If it could be shown that everything we can say about the world is primarily a result of our own human reason, then the justification of all our knowledge can no longer appeal merely to sense experi-ence or some other, higher-level form of knowledge. However, Kant's first, epistemological step demands proving that all other forms of human knowledge and action ulti-mately derive from constitutive acts of reason. It would have to be demonstrated that the essential commonalities in our cognitive understanding of our natural surroundings, as well as our moral actions and aesthetic perception are somehow the product of the human mind. Once we grasp this necessity, it becomes immediately clear that Kant's critique of reason would necessitate developing an entirely new philosophical system. The whole of the world, understood as comprising everything we are capable of knowing, would have to be shown to be a harmonious structure based on constitutive acts of reason. This pressure to understand philosophy as a systematic attempt to demonstrate the rationality of reality would become characteristic of German thought at the threshold of the nineteenth century.[5] For Kant, however, the

---

[5] See, among others, Eckart Förster, *Die 25 Jahre der Philosophie: Eine systematische Konstruktion* (Frankfurt: 2011), esp Part I;

task of philosophy first of all consisted in proving that our moral action is subject to principles of reason.

Although Kant would ultimately meet this challenge in an entirely independent fashion, along the way he would make use of a number of his immediate predecessors' insights. He would adopt Rousseau's proposal that acting morally means following autonomous rules and motives, for if we understood actions based on natural instincts as also being "moral", then we would have great difficulty distinguishing morally proper acts from the mere satisfaction of needs.[6] Yet, when it comes to how we should conceive of such individual self-determination, it is not Rousseau, but Adam Smith who plays godfather to Kant's solution. Although it is not well known, Kant did in fact borrow from the Scottish philosopher the idea that exercising moral self-control necessarily means judging our own actions from the perspective of an impartial observer. But even if we combine these two philosophical insights, we still will not have captured adequately the intention of Kant's *Critique of Practical Reason* (1788), which is that the proof that our moral action, just like our theoretical knowledge, is largely, if not exclusively, determined by reason. In order to prove this claim, Kant first needed to take an

Martin Heidegger, *Schelling's Treatise on the Nature of Human Freedom* (Athens, OH: Ohio University Press, 1985).

[6] Rousseau, *Social Contract*, p. 53; Immanuel Kant, *Groundwork of the Metaphysic of Morals* (Cambridge: Cambridge University Press), p. 3 (389), where Kant writes that a "precept, which is based on principles of mere experience – even if it is universal in a certain respect – insofar as it rests in the least part on empirical grounds, perhaps only in terms of a motive, can indeed be called a practical rule but never a moral law."

additional step that would carry him far beyond the work of both Rousseau and Smith. He claimed that the adoption of the perspective of an impartial observer, crucial for our moral autonomy, can only be adequately understood by conceiving of it as an act of submission to the demands of reason.[7] Although it is not mentioned explicitly, Kant thereby picks up on the same theoretical possibility that Smith had experimented with in his own considerations on the gradual expansion of the perspective of the impartial observer. Smith occasionally presumed that if this perspective were conceived of in a way that involved the concerns of all humans, there could hardly be any reason not to equate this perspective directly with reason.[8] Whereas Smith's empirical premises had prevented him from ultimately taking this step, Kant did not hesitate for a moment. For Kant, moral reason is identical to what is morally right from the perspective of all conceivable rational beings. Kant thereby arrived at the cornerstone of that part of his philosophical system which was dedicated to the powers of our practical reason. According to this part of his theory, we must view the powers of the human mind in this sphere of our actions as dictating to us the normative rules or "maxims" we must adhere to if we are to act morally.

This last conditional, however, points to a problem that Kant still had to solve. Up to this point he had only been able to demonstrate that subjects must adhere to the laws of moral reason once they have an inner willingness to do so, but

---

[7] See the famous formulations in Kant, *Groundwork*, pp. 13–15 (400–2).

[8] Smith, *Theory of Moral Sentiments*, p. 379.

he had not yet said anything about how subjects come to develop such a motive. It is at this point in his moral philosophy that the above-mentioned category of "respect" came into play, a term that will prove to be groundbreaking for the specifically German contribution to the modern discourse on recognition. Before Kant addresses this problem of motivation in his *Groundwork of the Metaphysics of Morals*, he introduces the category of "respect" by giving it a meaning that is less important for our purposes, one which indicates that morally motivated subjects' relation to the law of reason, which dictates the norms they follow, must be a relation of "respect".[9] This meaning hardly differs from what Hume and Smith must implicitly assume when claiming that subjects always respect the verdict of an impartial observer, which is necessary in order for them to be willing to restrict their own egotism. Of course, this use of the category of "respect" still does not solve the problem of why individuals should want to adhere to moral law at all. Here, when it comes to the motives for moral action, "respect" takes on a different meaning from what is relevant for the relation between subjects.

At this point, Kant must prove something that would in fact take him beyond the framework of his own system. In order to be able to name such a motive, he must form a connection between our empirical needs and the mental power he previously termed "reason". Previously it seemed as if Kant sought to conceive of the entirety of our moral action as being determined and constituted by reason. But if he is to make a claim about our motivation to act morally, he must go

9 Kant, *Groundwork*, p. 13 (400).

beyond this framework and establish some kind of connection between natural causality and the demands of reason. This is precisely the task of the expanded meaning he gives to "respect", thereby intending to show that we are "inclined" to show "respect" to other persons because we inevitably view them as exemplary embodiments of the efforts reason demands of us. Kant develops this bold notion in a relatively long footnote in his *Groundwork of the Metaphysics of Morals*, the significance of which for Kant's theory cannot be overestimated. First of all, we find here the idea that "respect" is a natural, but peculiar emotion; unlike all other natural emotions we cannot control or resist, "respect" is effected by reason itself:

> It could be objected that I only seek refuge, behind the word *respect*, in an obscure feeling, instead of distinctly resolving the question by means of a concept of reason. But though respect is a feeling, it is not one *received* by means of influence; it is, instead, a feeling *self-wrought* by means of a rational concept and therefore specifically different from all feelings of the first kind, which can be reduced to inclination or fear. . . . Respect is properly the representation of a worth that infringes upon my self-love.[10]

I view this last sentence as the key to understanding the somewhat puzzling formulation according to which an emotion is supposed to be "wrought" by reason; it means being so convinced, by virtue of a rational insight, of the

---

[10] Ibid., p. 14 (401), footnote.

value of an object that it produces an effect in our own emotions and needs, that is, a restriction of all our egocentric tendencies and intentions. "Respect" therefore merely means conceiving of the value of an object in a way that compels us to set aside our mere self-interest in order to do justice to the value of that object. Nevertheless, this does not yet explain what kind of object should be so valuable as to restrict our natural egocentric tendencies; and it is at this point that the relation to others finally comes to the fore.[11] Although Kant first of all writes in the same footnote that the object which compels such respect is the moral demand of reason or moral law, at the same time he seems to concede that such a law is not a perceptible object whose value we can grasp with our senses, thus going on to speak of other persons as embodying this law. The famous sentence in the footnote reads: "Any respect for a person is properly only respect for the law."[12]

---

[11] To be precise we would have to distinguish between two different layers of problems in Kant's passages on the concept of respect: first, the epistemological question of how we can assure ourselves of the existence of an object in the empirical world; and second, the moral-practical question of how the "feeling" of respect affects our capacity for reason in a way that compels us to act morally. Fichte attempted in his theory of natural law to answer the first question by claiming that the human face bears features of an "object" in the sensible world that demands our respect. See Johann Gottlieb Fichte, *Foundations of Natural Right* (Cambridge: Cambridge University Press, 2000), pp. 75–79. Some authors have attempted to draw connections between this passage and the ethical work of Emmanuel Levinas. See e.g. Simon Lumsden, "Absolute Difference and Social Ontology: Levinas Face to Face with Buber and Fichte", *Human Studies*, 3 (2000), pp. 227–41. (I owe these remarks to a detailed conversation with Michael Nance.)

[12] Kant, *Groundwork*, p. 14 (401), footnote.

At the core of this short sentence is the conception that other persons embody and exemplify the unconditional value of moral law restricting our self-interest. We respect others because they represent living examples of the effort required to follow the moral demands of reason. We could even say more pointedly that other persons allow us to experience sensually the value of moral law, because we can imagine their efforts adhering to this law. We thus feel compelled to respect other persons, because they do everything possible to meet the moral demands of reason in their everyday actions. If we relate this finding back to the problem of motivation that was the occasion for my turning to Kant's concept of "respect" in the first place, we will find his belief that we are motivated to submit to moral law because we encounter in other persons an object in the sensual world that compels us to "represent" a "worth" that "infringes upon my self-love".[13] What entirely abstract, rational moral law brings closer to human "intuition (by a certain analogy) and thereby to feeling", as Kant puts it in a wonderful passage of his *Groundwork for the Metaphysic of Morals*,[14] is the sensually perceptible insight that each person exemplifies a value that demands our respect and

---

[13] Of course, this interpretation gives Kant's solution to the problem of motivation an intersubjectivist turn. Generally, it is claimed that for Kant it is the respect for oneself as an end in itself, i.e. self-respect, that sufficiently motivates us to act morally. However, if we aim to show that Kant's concept of respect lays the groundwork for Hegel and Fichte's notion of recognition, we will have to emphasize the intersubjective tendency in Kant's solution. A number of Kant's strong formulations certainly seem to justify our doing so.

[14] Ibid., pp. 43 (436).

thus moves us to refrain from realizing our own mere ego-centric intentions.

This Kantian solution to the problem of moral motivation would prove groundbreaking for the idea of recognition that would soon establish itself in German Idealism. In two different senses, the concept of "respect" Kant draws upon in order to solve this problem establishes a bridge between subspheres of his system which otherwise would have had to remain strictly divided. First, respect for others is an epistemic act that is neither a pure, a priori act of reason nor a purely sensual experience. Instead, it represents or enables the perception in reality of empirical evidence for reason, such that in a peculiar way sensual perception and rational knowledge become identical. Second, however, the type of intellectual perception that respect represents for Kant is conceived of as having an effect on our empirical system of motivations, one which enables us to distance ourselves from our own self-referential inclinations. Respect for others thus effects a change in our nature by compelling us to grant the moral demands of reason priority over our own egocentric interests. Therefore, the concept of "respect" transgresses both the strict divide between the empirical and intelligible world as well as the divide between sensual perception and theoretical reasoning and knowledge. Moral reason can only motivate us if there is something in the human world of experience that bridges the gap between nature and mind. This is precisely what mutual respect is supposed to accomplish; Kant believes that we always already show each other respect because we see in each other the effort to realize moral law.

This bridge-building function is what made the Kantian concept of "respect" the theoretical pioneer for the idea of recognition prevalent in Germany. Both representatives of German Idealism who would go on to establish this concept and give it systematic significance – Fichte and Hegel – see this restriction of our self-interest, which Kant regarded as characteristic for interpersonal "respect", as the main feature of all recognition. Furthermore, they adopt Kant's idea that recognition or respect mediates between human nature and mind, because it represents both a kind of "intellectual perception" as well as a shift in our natural system of needs. However, both of these philosophers would transplant these determinations of recognition into a rational philosophical system that is fundamentally different from that of Kant.

Before I address the formation of this specifically German contribution to the idea of recognition, I will have to examine another aspect of Kant's concept of "respect". Up to this point, we have not yet been able to determine how this concept supports the idea that all citizens should in principle be equal. This normative feature of Kant's concept of respect can only be understood adequately by comparing it to the views of recognition already discussed in the intellectual context of France and Great Britain at the onset of modernity.

What immediately becomes apparent is that a need for social esteem or recognition plays absolutely no role whatsoever in Kant's moral philosophy. He conceives of "respect" in terms of a subject compelled by its peers to show respect, but not in terms of a subject that has or feels a desire to receive respect. Kant does occasionally address the individual's desire for privilege or greater social status; throughout his writings on the philosophy of history, for instance, we find the idea, influenced by Rousseau's concept of "amour propre", that we can hypothetically assume the progress of human culture by assuming that the individual's desire for social rank constantly produces theoretical and moral progress.[15] For reasons that are quite clear and are linked to the systemic nature of Kant's concept of practical reason, however, such a profane, egocentric motivation cannot play any motivational role. In Kant's eyes it would be absurd to regard the validity of moral demands as being a result of the inclinations of needy humans; the latter are supposed to be enabled to restrict their self-interest by virtue of rational insight. Therefore, the motif of recognition found in Kant's concept of "respect" is entirely different from what we find in the cultural contexts we have reviewed thus far. At least within the framework of his theory of morality, Kant does not have in mind a kind of recognition desired by a needy subject, but rather the kind of recognition we pay or owe to others. It is not until Hegel comes along that we once again encounter the idea of a "need for recognition"; however, unlike the tradition of "amour propre", Hegel does not address a psychological but a "spiritual" desire – one which requires further elucidation.[16]

---

[15] See Axel Honneth, "The Irreducibility of Progress: Kant's Account of the Relationship Between Morality and History", *Critical Horizons*, vol. 8, no. 1 (2007), pp. 1–17.

[16] See pp. 129–130 in this book.

At any rate Kant conceives of "respect" solely as an emotional stance that becomes almost inevitable once we properly employ our powers of judgment on others. When we encounter another subject in this way, we must grasp it almost automatically as an exemplary embodiment of moral law. For that reason, we are moved immediately to restrict our self-interest and take up a respectful attitude. Any additional meanings Kant goes on to ascribe to the concept of "respect" derive in principle from this initial determination. First, the fact that we are compelled to thus perceive all other subjects implies the universal reciprocity of equal respect; as soon as we have learned to recognize the workings of moral law in *one* other subject, we will have to show the same moral respect to *all* other subjects. Second, for Kant this kind of respect entails that we grant others the individual freedom to determine their own ends and therefore enjoy autonomy. After all, such respect is supposed to coincide with a restriction of "my self-love", such that I must set aside my own interests in order to grant others the autonomy to determine their own life aims. Once we combine these two conclusions, we get the claim, so crucial to Kant's moral philosophy, that all human beings, as intelligent creatures, are mutually obligated to respect each other's right to autonomy.

Just how liberating the core of Kant's moral rationalism proved to be to relatively backward Germany can be seen in the fact that there was hardly a young scholar or philosopher who was not influenced by it. The categorical imperative found in Kant's *Critique of Practical Reason* would soon be perceived in all university and intellectual circles as the demand to emancipate ourselves once and for all from the domination of the feudal nobility and to struggle to achieve moral equality for all citizens.[17] Marx' famous claim that Germans were only capable of fighting for the revolution intellectually which the French had won on the streets[18] applies much more to Kant than to Hegel, to whom Marx' claim was actually addressed. Within the space of only a few years, the Königsberg philosopher would bring about a revolution of moral "thinking" in Germany that would provide a justification, anchored in our capacity for reason, for the revolutionary demand for equal respect. Nevertheless, the concept of "respect", the external side of Kant's moral rationalism, stood on extremely unsteady ground. This sentiment clearly represented a mixture – half empirical claim and half rational obligation, without there being any clear connection between the two. On the one hand, all human beings are supposed to be automatically respectful as soon as they encounter another subject; on the other hand, this respect seems only to come into effect when the other can be categorized as a moral being owing to a particular form of his powers of

---

[17] A striking impression of this liberating effect of Kant's ethics can be found – though in language that might seem a bit too flowery today – in Harmann August Korff in his monumental work *Der Geist der Goethezeit*, 4 vols (Leipzig: Koehler & Amelang, 1927–30), here vol. 2, p. 202ff. On more recent accounts, see Frederick C. Beiser, *Enlightenment, Revolution, and Romanticism: The Genesis of Modern German Political Thought 1790–1800* (Cambridge, MA: Harvard University Press, 1992), ch. 2.

[18] Karl Marx, "A Contribution to the Critique of Hegel's Philosophy of Right: Introduction", in *Karl Marx: Early Writings* (New York: Vintage, 1975), pp. 243–57.

judgment.[19] Hardly any of the younger philosophers who sang the praises of Kant's moral rationalism failed to recognize that this strange ambiguity represented a serious weakness in his moral-philosophical approach. The attempt of this admired thinker to anchor the laws of ethics in human beings' system of motivations with the aid of the concept of respect would soon come to be viewed as a helpless, unconvincing back-and-forth between empirical claims and transcendental speculation.[20] One of the more important functions of the concept of "recognition" put forth by Fichte, and later by Hegel, therefore consisted in resolving this grave theoretical deficit. The German idea of recognition is thus rooted in the effort to find a more convincing alternative to Kant's conception of the motives for moral action.

In principle, those dissatisfied with Kant's account of the motivating role of respect could choose between two different paths of correction. The ambivalence in Kant's concept of "respect" could be resolved either in empirical or in intelligible terms, that is, either by taking the path laid down

---

[19] On the problem and the system of Kant's concept of respect, see the very illuminating study by Steffi Schadow, *Achtung für das Gesetz: Moral und Motivation bei Kant* (Berlin: de Gruyter, 2012).

[20] On the significance of this problem of motivation in the work of Kant, see also: Andreas Wildt, *Autonomie und Anerkennung: Hegels Moralitätskritik im Lichte seiner Fichte-Rezeption* (Stuttgart: Klett-Cotta, 1982), pp. 165–73; Dieter Henrich, "Die Deduktion des Sittengesetzes: Über die Gründe der Dunkelheit des letzten Abschnitts von Kants 'Grundlegung zur Metaphysik der Sitten'", in Alexander Schwan, ed., *Denken im Schatten des Nihilismus: Festschrift für W. Weischedel* (Darmstadt: Wissenschaftliche Buchgesellschaft, 1975), pp. 55–112.

by Scottish moral philosophy or by seeking out an entirely independent solution. In the first case, respect would have to be made into an object of all human striving in order to grasp it as the source of the desire for moral agreement with others. In the second case, a rational motive necessarily compelling all humans to respect certain moral principles would have to be found. The fact that Fichte and Hegel did not hesitate to rule out the first path and choose the second one was a result of their far-reaching agreement with the premise of the Kantian system, according to which all of reality is ultimately based on rationality. Unlike their predecessor, these two younger thinkers immediately sought to prove that the rationality of the real could not merely be the product of our rational knowledge, but had to be a real object – such that the entirety of the world had to be understood as a result of the activity of reason.[21] Therefore, the idea of taking the path of British moral philosophy and searching for empirical, profane motives for moral action was unimaginable to both Fichte and Hegel. If they wanted to offer a more convincing alternative to Kant's solution of the problem of motivation, they would have to find motives for moral action grounded in our own mental, spiritual activity.[22] The concept of "recognition" which Fichte and Hegel would soon develop in each of their

[21] Paul Guyer, "Absolute Idealism and the Rejection of Kantian Dualism", in Karl Ameriks, ed., *The Cambridge Companion to German Idealism* (Cambridge: Cambridge University Press, 2000), pp. 37–56.

[22] An independent attempt to solve Kant's motivation problem can be found in Friedrich Schiller, "On Grace and Dignity", in Jane Curran and Christophe Fricker, eds, *Schiller's "On Grace and Dignity" in Its Cultural Context: Essays and a New Translation"* (Rochester: Camden House,

respective philosophical systems had the task of solving precisely this intricate problem.

Johann Gottlieb Fichte, eight years Hegel's senior, launched his own attack on Kant by making the bold claim that the formation of the objective world should not be viewed as a mere cognitive act, but as the tangible, practical act of an always already acting ego. Taking his point of departure in the idealist principle he developed for the first time in his *Wissenschaftslehre* (*Doctrine of Scientific Knowledge*) in 1794,[23] he sketched the process by which such an "absolute ego" attempts to realize its autonomy by employing its own reason and gradually reshaping the material it has created. We need not concern ourselves with Fichte's methodological justification or with his execution of his systematic project; what is relevant for our purposes is the point at which he saw a need to address the plurality of human individuals by addressing their relation to each other. This is the point when an active ego's efforts to attain autonomy force it to become conscious of its always already "free activity". Fichte was convinced that this is an act that the subject, previously conceived of as "absolute", can no longer perform on its own, because its previously shaped and reshaped material offers no indication of what it means to be capable of free "self-activity". At this

---

2005), pp. 123–70. See also Wildt, *Autonomie und Anerkennung*, pp. 157–62.

[23] Johann Gottlieb Fichte, *Grundlage der gesamten Wissenschaftslehre* [1794], in *Fichtes Werke*, vol. 1, pp. 83–328. See also Frederick Neuhouser, *Fichte's Theory of Subjectivity* (Cambridge: Cambridge University Press, 1990).

point in the development of his system, therefore, Fichte could no longer speak in the singular of the subject which actively realizes itself in the use of its reason, rather only in the plural. If the self-realizing subject did not encounter other, similar beings, it would be incapable of becoming conscious of its own, free "self-activity". We will set aside the obvious question of whether Fichte really intended this step toward the intersubjectivity of a plurality of individuals as a revision of his own starting point: an isolated, transcendental subject. Even today there is debate on the solution to this problem, without the result having much effect on the understanding of the interaction Fichte goes on to describe.[24] Fichte essentially dedicates an entire book to the subject's encounter of another subject in the external world; its title is *Foundations of Natural Right* and can be regarded as the founding document of the specifically German idea of recognition.[25]

The very title of this influential work shows that Fichte would go on to present the relation between subjects as a legal relation. But before he could arrive at this conclusion, he first had to give an account of what presumably goes on in the consciousness of the subject once it encounters another subject. Fichte employed the method of transcendental deduction he adopted from Kant, according to which

[24] On the significance of this problem, see Axel Honneth, "Die transzendentale Notwendigkeit von Intersubjektivität: Zum zweiten Lehrsatz in Fichtes Naturrechtsabhandlung", in *Unsichtbarkeit: Stationen einer Theorie der Intersubjektivität* (Frankfurt: Suhrkamp, 2003), pp. 28–48, here pp. 47f.

[25] Fichte, *Foundations of Natural Right.*

it is possible to uncover step by step the necessary conditions of the possibility of self-consciousness.[26] The step of this deduction relevant for our purposes is introduced by the observation that a subject which desires to become conscious of its own "free self-determination to exercise efficacy" cannot perform such an act of self-cognition as long as it is only faced with non-conscious material. The subject can set goals that allow it to shape and reshape nature in accordance with its own ideas, but this decision for free, self-determined activity cannot enable the subject to acquire an adequate picture of its own act of will. Fichte thus concluded that the subject must take a further step in order to arrive at self-consciousness in the sense of having a notion of its own capacity for self-determined activity.[27] At this point in his deduction, Fichte fundamentally altered the framework of his own account by suddenly placing the subject among other subjects. In brief, as an observing philosopher, he asked how the subject's self-perception would change once suddenly faced with the presence of a similar being. Such an external subject encounters the subject by receiving a kind of "summons". An individual reflectively concerned with its own relation to the objects it shapes and reshapes is suddenly "summoned", such that it can be certain of being the addressee of an utterance.

The concept of the "summons" employed by Fichte in order to characterize this first appearance of the other should in no way be understood as a demand or command.

---

[26] See again Neuhouser, *Fichte's Theory of Subjectivity*, pp. 93–102.

[27] Fichte, *Foundations of Natural Right*, pp. 30–9.

As Allen Wood has shown convincingly in a recent book,[28] Fichte intended this summons instead as an invitation of another subject to do something that we can either do or not do. Fichte's analysis of this communicative situation focused primarily on the interpretive acts the addressee must perform in order to understand the summons of another subject as being just such an invitation to act. First, the addressee must be able to distinguish the imperatives of natural causality from those represented by such a summons. This second kind of causality, which cannot be conceived of as a relation of cause and effect, but only functions by means of an appeal to "reason", already presupposes "a being capable of having concepts"[29] as the source of its causality. In order to understand such a summons, therefore, we must presuppose knowledge of the existence of another rational, intentional subject. Yet the addressee would still not have understood completely what makes a summons a summons if they were only to remain aware of the rationality of the summoner. According to Fichte it must at the same time be able to realize that its partner in interaction assumes that its addressee is a rational being capable of understanding, and thus of acting freely. Fichte sees the second condition of understanding a "summons" in the addressee's understanding of this summons as an utterance that demands a free reaction.[30]

---

[28] Allen Wood, *The Free Development of Each: Studies on Freedom, Right, and Ethics in Classical German Philosophy* (Oxford: Oxford University Press, 2014), p. 207.

[29] Fichte, *Foundations of Natural Right*, p. 35. [30] Ibid., p. 37.

Up to this point in his transcendental deduction, however, Fichte does not use the term "recognition" at all. So it is not yet apparent why this should be a superior solution to the problem of motivation which Kant sought to solve by introducing the feeling of respect. Fichte does not undertake such a solution until the next step, asking what else the summoned subject can know about another rational being. His answer is brief, but in his eyes it suffices to explain our motivation to act morally. A subject must know that the speaker addressing it has been willing to restrict its own freedom, for by summoning another subject and thus expecting a free reaction, it must be willing to make room for the interests of its addressees. It is no accident, therefore, that Fichte repeatedly mentions the willing restriction of one's own freedom;[31] in a clear reference to Kant, who also saw respect as a feeling that "impinges upon my self-love",[32] Fichte refers to the "summons" as an implicit expression of respect. In Fichte's view, calling upon someone to act always also means showing respect for that person, for the act of summoning presupposes that we refrain from asserting our own, private freedom. Yet, even at this point, Fichte still does not use the term "recognition"; his argument still needs to take another turn, directing our attention back toward the addressed subject. Fichte claims that this subject must also restrict its own freedom if it wishes to adequately respond to being summoned. Because the other's utterance is intended to move the addressee to act freely, the latter must signal that it has adequately understood this summoning by willingly restricting its own private freedom in turn. It is at this point

---

[31] Ibid., p. 41. [32] Kant, *Groundwork*, p. 14 (401), footnote.

that we find the words Fichte famously used to coin the idea of recognition in the German-speaking context: "One cannot recognize the other if both do not mutually recognize each other; and one cannot treat the other as a free being if both do not mutually treat each other as free."[33]

This sentence could be seen as a motto for the particularly German conception of recognition following Fichte and Hegel, after whom many would attempt to conceive of intersubjective relations in terms of such reciprocity in the recognition of "free beings". For Fichte himself, however, this sentence was nothing more than an intermediate step summarizing his previous findings in his deduction of the conditions of the possibility of self-consciousness. In the next step of his argumentation, he gives an account of why this reciprocity can be regarded as the foundation of all legal relations.[34] Yet, for our purposes, Fichte's account is already sufficient to understand why he regards his idea of recognition as a superior alternative to Kant's solution to the problem of motivation. If we look back at his analysis, we see that Fichte felt it necessary to introduce a second subject into his analysis of the conditions of self-consciousness, for without the presence of another rational being, the subject would not be capable of getting sight of its

---

[33] Fichte, *Foundations of Natural Right*, pp. 42ff. At this point, however, we should note that Fichte, in contrast to how Kant treats the concept of "respect", does not employ the term "recognition" as an "emotion". For Fichte, what is important about this "restriction" of self-interest is primarily the "expressive" side, while he gives no indication of whether this must be regarded as being connected with a certain emotional state. (I owe this observation, too, to Michael Nance.)

[34] Ibid., §4.

own mental acts. Fichte explained how a subject that strives for self-consciousness becomes aware of the presence of a second subject by claiming the existence of an intersubjective "summons", thereby ultimately referring to everyday speech acts through which one person seeks to invite or motivate another person to act. At this point Fichte's entire analysis focuses on the necessary conditions for interacting subjects' ability to adequately understand each other. He was convinced that the summoning of one subject by another will induce a shift in the attitude of both subjects, which in turn radically changes their respective self-understanding, because they must mutually understand each other. Fichte claimed that as soon as the summoning subject performs a speech act, it must "impinge on its own self-love", because it inevitably grants its addressee the freedom to determine how it wishes to react. Fichte makes essentially the same claim about the summoned subject. It, too, must "impinge on its self-love" because it can only show that it has understood the summoning by granting the speaker the freedom to react to its own reaction. When it comes to the moral act, which, according to Fichte, both subjects must perform in order to understand each other adequately, it is no accident that I havè already used Kant's term "respect", according to which it represents a willing restriction of one's "own self-love". This should demonstrate Fichte's claim that such mutual respect is a condition of the possibility of the mutual understanding of the speech act called "summoning". We are thus justified in concluding that Fichte sought to prove that the interpersonal respect that Kant drew upon to explain our motivation to act morally already represents a necessary condition of understanding communicative utterances.

If we return to Fichte's original reason for introducing such a communicative situation, then it follows that a stance of moral respect is a condition of the possibility of self-consciousness. Only if a subject enters into a communicative relationship of mutual recognition can it experience itself spontaneously as a rationally active being, seeing the other as a mirror of its own activity.[35] Before I compare this idea of recognition to the previously explained conceptions of intersubjectivity, I want to explain briefly why it represents a serious alternative to Kant's solution to the problem of motivation. Fichte and, a bit later, Hegel were both convinced that Kant did not manage to explain why humans should be motivated to follow rational demands of morality. Both were suspicious of the notion that we should rely on an emotion that occupied an ambiguous position between natural causality and rational knowledge. Fichte sought to resolve this divide in conformity with his own systematic conception by locating the motivation to act morally in a subject's efforts to realize itself through acts of active reason in a self-created reality. He maintained that such a rational self-motivation arises once the subject is suddenly faced with having to respond appropriately to the summoning of another subject, i.e. to being addressed by others. Fichte believed that the addressed subject will be compelled to show respect to the speaker, for it must thereby demonstrate that it has understood the other's utterance as an invitation to react autonomously. Therefore, for Fichte, respect or recognition of the other as

---

[35] On a more precise elucidation of this condition of self-consciousness, see Honneth, "Die transzendentale Notwendigkeit von Intersubjektivität"; see also Wildt, *Autonomie und Anerkennung"*, ch. II.4.

a "free being" represents an element of every speaking interaction inasmuch as it encourages or invites us to react in a free, self-determined way. No "emotion" is needed to motivate the addressee to show moral respect; its own mental effort to interpret another person's speech act is enough to motivate such respect. A little more than a century and a half later, this idea would be revisited in German philosophy by Karl Otto Apel, whose discourse ethics is likewise based on the idea that speech acts can only be understood if the speakers recognize each other as equal and free beings.[36]

Just as vast as the gap between the French and the British conception of interpersonal encounters is the gap between Fichte's concept of recognition and these two conceptual worlds. Of course, this divide is largely due to the fact that Fichte, in his attempt to outdo Kant, developed a philosophical system with which he aimed to prove that the entire world is a product of the rational activity of a constituting subject. He therefore regarded the efforts of French and British thinkers to decode the meaning of intersubjective encounters, the French with psychological means and the British with empirical means, as too weak. Anyone seriously looking to understand the meaning of human encounters would, in Fichte's view, have to adequately grasp the totalizing power of our reason. This is

---

[36] Karl-Otto Apel, *Diskurs und Verantwortung: Das Problem des Übergangs zur postkonventionellen Moral* (Frankfurt: Suhrkamp, 1988); on Fichte, see pp. 445ff. With regard to Apel's relation to Fichte, see Vittorio Hösle, *Die Krise der Gegenwart und die Verantwortung der Philosophie* (Munich: Beck, 1977), esp. pp. 220ff. See also Wolfgang Kuhlmann, *Reflexive Letztbegründung: Untersuchungen zur Tranzendentalpragmatik* (Freiburg: Alber, 1985).

precisely what Fichte intended by concluding that we always already recognize each other reciprocally as "free beings", because our "reason" compels us to understand adequately the summoning utterance of the other. We can only do so if we have realized that we have only been called upon to act because a free and unforced reaction has been asked of us. By taking this rational-philosophical step, Fichte places a variable at the center of his analysis of subjectivity that had played almost no role at all in the debates we have recounted thus far. The social value of the individual is not what is at stake when it encounters others, nor is it called upon to exercise moral self-control when it strives for social relationships; rather, this kind of communication is what in a certain way makes the subject into a free being in the first place. Of course Fichte was aware of something like the natural freedom of rational beings, which consists in the impetuous desire to completely realize our own rational capacities in a (self-produced) reality; yet, this freedom does not become a proven fact to our consciousness until we are forced to restrict it in our encounters with other, likewise rational beings, to whom we seek to prove our rationality. For Fichte, therefore, what brings about the intersubjective encounter of recognition is the transformation of a merely natural, spontaneous freedom into a shared reality of secure claims to self-determination.

The price that Fichte had to pay for his interpretation of intersubjective communication is quite high. Unlike the thinkers we have discussed thus far, Fichte could not so easily adapt his conception of communication to empirical reality. Whereas his predecessors – whether Rousseau, Hume or Smith – had always based their analyses on actual facts of everyday interaction, the only part of such interactions that remained for Fichte were those which could occur within the consciousness of rationally acting beings. He did later make numerous attempts to render such idealizing determinations of recognition more plausible in terms of our actions in the lifeworld; for instance, he noted that mutual recognition is empirically exemplified by the educational process, because adults must inevitably address the still immature child as a "free being" in order to unleash the latter's potential for self-determination.[37] Moreover, Fichte's attempt to conceive of the "civil contract" [Staatsbürgervertrag] as an expression of intersubjective recognition represented a further effort to lend transcendental events a stronger anchoring in historical reality.[38] Yet, even these attempts at empirical concretization do little to refute the suspicion that Fichte's model of recognition ultimately fails to refer to subjects of flesh and blood. His argumentation remains too much within the Kantian world of intelligible beings to have a lasting effect on how we understand the meaning of intersubjective relationships.[39] In fact, perhaps Fichte's few remarks on the reciprocity of recognition would never have had any influence on German-speaking philosophy at all had they not inspired Hegel to develop his own, far more empirically substantial concept of recognition.

Hegel integrated the impulses he gained by studying Fichte's work on "Natural Right" into a methodological

---

[37] Fichte, *Foundations of Natural Right*, p. 38 ("The summons to engage in free activity is what we call 'upbringing' [*Erziehung*]").

[38] Ibid., §17.

[39] Given the strong emphasis that Fichte places on human needs and on the corporeality of humans as "finite beings" in his discussion of natural right, this formulation might seem very unfair. It is only meant to apply, however, to Fichte's model of recognition.

framework which would subsequently allow him to lend concrete substance to the previously abstract act of mutual recognition. He rejected Kant and Fichte's division between an "empirical" and an "intelligible" world, developing his own system: a phenomenology of self-realizing spirit. Hegel no longer sought to investigate the transcendental conditions needed to allow human reason to realize itself, aiming instead at a "phenomenological" understanding of the steps by which spirit frees itself from all natural determinations in order to become completely autonomous. Therefore, every element of his system must correspond to something in the real world, for it is there that spirit is to realize itself. On the basis of this fundamental shift in systematic perspective,[40] the young philosopher attempted already during his time in Jena to appropriate Fichte's model of recognition in a way that allows us to recognize the worldly features of events which are nevertheless constitutive for the formation of spirit. According to Hegel, the love between a man and a woman enables us to see what it means to recognize each other as "free beings" in the everyday dealings of concrete humans.[41]

If we were to summarize Hegel's argumentation and translate it into a more modern language, we could say that to love someone means to recognize their desires and interests as reasons to restrict our own actions, because we experience

---

[40] On Hegel's systematic perspective, see Dina Emundts and Rolf-Peter Horstmann, *G. W. F. Hegel: Eine Einführung* (Stuttgart: Reclam, 2002), esp. pp. 32ff.

[41] On the systematic role of "love" in early Hegel, see Dieter Henrich, "Hegel and Hölderlin", in *Hegel im Kontext* (Frankfurt: Suhrkamp, 1971), pp. 9–40.

them as being worthy of our support and care. If we conceive of this form of moral self-restriction in favor of the other as a reciprocal occurrence, as is usually the case when it comes to love, we find a social form of the very same structure of mutual recognition Fichte ascribed solely to his "transcendental" figures. The two lovers restrict their own self-interest in favor of the respective other in order to foster that which they each regard as worthy of love in the other. This, however, only explains why the young Hegel believed that "respect", whose interpretation caused Kant so much difficulty, occurs in love almost as a matter of fact. What we still have not clarified is why this form of reciprocal recognition in love should also produce the freedom of the other. The key to Hegel's answer to this question is found in his famous formula according to which forms of reciprocal recognition such as love represent modes of "being with oneself in another".[42] If the value in which one person sees itself recognized by another is an important part of that person's own self-understanding, then that person will understand the recognizing reaction of the other as a public confirmation of its own self, thereby granting the latter validity in the objective world. When it comes to love, therefore, Hegel viewed the experience of "being recognized" as the feeling of being "free" to determine the elements of one's own subjectivity that are publicly

---

[42] In the section on "Logic" in the *Encyclopedia*, Hegel defines "freedom" as "being with oneself in another": G. W. F. Hegel, *Encyclopedia of the Philosophical Sciences in Basic Outline* (Cambridge: Cambridge University Press, 2010), p. 60. We find this formulation in somewhat altered form in many of Hegel's other works, often referring to events of mutual recognition.

esteemed by virtue of the other's self-restriction in a secure, "conscious" way. According to Hegel, therefore, three conditions need to be fulfilled in order for recognition to bring about individual freedom. It must be reciprocal, consist in complementary self-restriction and have an expressive, i.e. generally accessible and perceptible, character.

Certainly, this is not the language Hegel employed in his Jena sketches to interpret love as an already existing example of the kind of mutual recognition that Fichte sought to characterize transcendentally and thus import it into the sphere of intelligible beings. The young Hegel's turn away from Fichte's transcendentalism represents a departure from the effort to interpret recognition as an occurrence between two conscious subjects, regarding it instead as the result of the unifying power of spirit, which resolves antagonisms and produces a living universal by means of love.[43] But regardless of whether we account for this step in an internal or external manner, this early line of thought shows that Hegel employed the idea of "recognition" unlike any of the other thinkers I have discussed thus far. Whereas Rousseau, Sartre, Hume, Smith, and even Fichte had sought to uncover the basic normative features of all human communication, Hegel limited his analysis to a few specific forms of communication as the sole examples of what he termed "recognition". We could therefore say that Hegel's concept of "recognition" is thoroughly normative; he was not concerned with general, invariant structures of social interaction, nor with whether every human encounter in fact mobilizes "amour propre" or an "impartial spectator".

[43] See Henrich, "Hegel and Hölderlin".

What Hegel had in mind are instead historically given configurations of human intersubjectivity produced by spirit and fulfilling the three above-mentioned conditions. These configurations must be institutionalized, and thus "real" or "objective", forms of human communication in which subjects restrict their respective self-interest by "expressively" showing their respect for each other as equals in their being-for-itself. If this is true, then Hegel seems to assume that subjects can experience that which they previously experienced as merely private freedom as a universally approved, "objective" claim to self-determination.

Yet, the very fact that Hegel, at first, only regarded "love" as a realization of recognition shows that his intellectual development was not yet complete. The further he developed his system and the more he realized that in order to grasp the processual realization of spirit in nature and history he must inquire into entirely different areas of reality, the more relative the objective status of love becomes.[44] Hegel arrived at a further threshold in the development of his system once he undertook his "philosophy of the objective spirit", thereby accounting for the realization of the spirit in institutionalized social life. After making the requisite changes to his basic categories, Hegel saw himself compelled to put a much greater social-theoretical emphasis on recognition as a guarantor of freedom. Two changes in particular result from this social-theoretical expansion of Hegel's account of recognition. First, Hegel assumed that the value a recognizing

---

[44] See Axel Honneth, *The Struggle for Recognition: The Moral Grammar of Social Conflicts* (Cambridge, MA: MIT Press, 1995), p. 38.

subject sees in the other does not merely represent an individual preference, but rather conveys the social order of preferences in which mutually recognizing subjects have been raised. "Objective spirit" – i.e. the particular set of institutions that have become "second nature" – is what decides which desires and interests individuals have and which facets of subjectivity they thus learn to admire in each other. In his *Philosophy of Right*, Hegel concluded from this "sociological" turn that modern society is home to three ethical spheres (the family, civil society and the state) with specific conditions of mutual recognition in the above-mentioned normative sense – provided that society is organized in a rational manner.[45]

With his insight into the institutional mediation of all processes of recognition, Hegel came to recognize that such acts of mutual recognition can lead to social conflicts if the prevalent social value order causes individuals to ascribe to each other unequal normative characteristics. In this case struggles can arise over which of their subjective capacities are truly valuable and should thus call for restricting one's own actions by means of recognizing the other. In the famous chapter on "master and slave" in

---

[45] A deficit in the history of sociology is that it has failed to take proper account of Hegel's formative role for the emergence of this discipline in the nineteenth century. Generally, only Montesquieu, Rousseau, Condorcet, Ferguson, Smith and occasionally Herder are counted among the "philosophical forerunners" of sociology. See Robert Bierstedt, "Sociological Thought in the Eighteenth Century", in Tom Bottomore and Robert Nisbet, eds, *A History of Sociology* (London: Rawat, 1979), pp. 3–38.

Hegel's *Phenomenology of Spirit*, which immediately follows his first mentioning of mutual recognition as
a necessary condition of an objectively guaranteed consciousness of freedom, Hegel systematically treated this
conflict-laden side of his theory for the first time. He
claimed that a master and its slave cannot manage to reciprocally affirm each other's respective being-for-itself,
because the social norms which provide the horizon for
their actions do not permit such a symmetrical self-
recognition in the typical social characteristics of the
other.[46]

Such connections might allow us to claim that Hegel
assumed the existence of a "need" or "desire" for recognition,
even though he did not explicitly formulate the matter in this
way. Alexander Kojève first brought this expression to promi-
nence by placing it at the center of his interpretation of the
chapter on "master and slave" in his famous lectures on the
Phenomenology of Spirit, in which he interpreted the "desire"
for "the desire of the other" as a specifically human need for
recognition.[47] Kojève did not, however, give us a clear sense of
what could be meant by such a "need",[48] and even today there
are many interpreters who speak of such a desire without
asking what Hegel could have meant by such an expression.[49]

[46] G. W. F. Hegel, *Phenomenology of Spirit* (Oxford: Oxford University
Press, 1977), part IV, A, pp. 111–19.
[47] Alexandre Kojève, *Introduction to the Reading of Hegel: Lectures on the
Phenomenology of Spirit* (Ithaca: Cornell University Press, 1969), p. 6.
[48] See Wildt, *Autonomie und Anerkennung*, p. 354.
[49] Judith Butler, who is clearly a disciple of Kojève (see her book *Subjects of
Desire: Hegelian Reflections in Twentieth-Century France* (New York:

It is obvious that the author of the *Phenomenology of Spirit* and the *Philosophy of Right* did not have in mind just any empirical tendency, sensual need or natural desire. Such factual desires play an important role in Hegel's construction of "objective spirit", as he believed that every social order must always also be capable of satisfying our given, historically refined needs; but when it comes to "recognition", he could not have meant an object of the natural, sensual desire of subjects, for recognition is desired for the sake of realizing our rational subjectivity. It would be misleading to suggest any association with the meaning of recognition in the work of Rousseau, Hume or Smith when they speak of the desire for social status. When Hegel spoke of a "need" for recognition, he had in mind a kind of striving that reaches much deeper into the intellectual constitution of human subjectivity, and that must refer to a kind of rational desire to lend objective expression to our capacity for free self-determination. Hegel must presuppose that every human subject possesses not only sensual inclinations but also the more profound desire to realize in the external world the freedom that constitutes the most inner experience of subjectivity. Furthermore, Hegel must assume that in order to be able to satisfy this desire, we require an institutionally

Columbia University Press, 2012), esp. ch. 2), occasionally employs a Spinozian idea by locating the source of a "need" for recognition in the drive ("conatus") for social self-preservation: Judith Butler, *The Psychic Life of Power: Theories in Subjection* (Stanford: Stanford University Press, 1997), p. 62. We see an even more problematic conflation of Hegel's "need" for recognition with Spinoza's drive for self-preservation in " Beside Oneself: On the Limits of Sexual Autonomy", in *Undoing Gender* (London: Routledge, 2004), pp. 17–38, here p. 31.

organized system of recognition by others, who, by restricting their own self-interests, publicly express their support for the self-determination of others.

It becomes apparent, therefore, that at the point where Hegel seemed to come closest to the notion of recognition cultivated by the previous philosophical tradition, i.e. his mention of a "need" for recognition, the difference between him and his predecessors was all the greater. Whereas Rousseau, Hume and Smith had interpreted this need with slightly different accentuations as a sensual desire, i.e. as something that Kant generally viewed as the epitome of our "inclinations",[50] Hegel, the offspring of German Idealism, viewed this as an interest of our reason in itself, in its own realization. He grasped the "need" for recognition as the desire to realize our ability for a kind of rational self-determination that desires to be free and undisturbed. Certainly, Hegel must also make the causal effectiveness of such a "spiritual" desire empirically plausible so as to prevent it from being a mere chimera. This explains the many passages in which he referred to sensual embodiments of this need in the real world of social occurrences. On such occasions he obviously had in mind the efforts of historically situated subjects seeking to either expand their sphere of self-determination or to be included in institutionally established relations of recognition. Hegel, however, aimed to capture more than what is generally indicated by such expressions. He referred not only to the sensual need to be free from this or that obstacle, but to

---

[50] Kant, *Groundwork*, p. 81 (413, footnote): "The dependence of the power of appetition on sensations is called an inclination, and thus an inclination always indicates a *need.*"

the desire, dictated to us by reason, to practice our own capacity for self-determination as freely as possible.

Hegel, inspired by Fichte, thus gave the Kantian concept of "respect" both an intersubjectivist and a historical spin. When two subjects encounter each other in institutionally organized relations of recognition formed as a result of the historical process of "progress in the consciousness of freedom", each offers the other a particular form of "respect", because they have been socialized to obey the norms on which this respect is founded. If these subjects come to view relations of recognition as being too narrow, too constricting or too unequal, Hegel is convinced that the constant force of our rational will for self-determination will necessarily lead to struggles for new, expanded forms of recognition.

Now, it would certainly be wrong to want to claim that precisely this demanding version of Hegel's ideas would make his work the vehicle of a specifically German idea of recognition. Neither his sociological nor his historical turn would be immediately and adequately understood, and for a time only the leftovers of his claim of a human desire for mutual recognition would remain. In this extremely reduced form, however, Hegel's concept of recognition would have an enormous amount of influence on intellectual development in Germany – as much on the thought of Brecht as on the philosophy of dialog arising at the beginning of the twentieth century.[51] The guiding idea in

---

[51] See Bertolt Brecht, "Mr. Puntila and his Man Matti", in *Brecht Collected Plays: Six* (London: Bloomsbury, 2001). See also Hans Mayer, "Hegels 'Herr und Knecht' in der modernen Literatur (Hofmannsthal – Brecht – Beckett)", *Stuttgarter Hegel-Tage 1970: Vorträge und Kolloquien des Internationalen Hegel-Kongresses*, ed.

both cases was that every intersubjective encounter between humans is marked by the mutual expectation that we be treated as equal among equals, which is why any violation of this equality would inevitably cause conflicts to arise. Even the way in which the class struggle came to be theorized was often dominated by the notion of a drama between master and slave, a systematically distorted or disturbed relationship of mutual recognition.[52] However, we will not get a complete sense of the complex structure of Hegel's theory of recognition until the following, concluding chapter. Here I will attempt to provide a systematic summary of my historical reconstruction.

Hans-Georg Gadamer (Bonn: Meiner, 1974), pp. 53–78. On the philosophy of dialog see Michael Theunissen, *Der Andere: Studien zur Sozialontologie der Gegenwart* (Berlin and New York: Campus, 1977), part II, esp. pp. 473f.

[52] See e.g. Hans Heinz Holz, *Herr und Knecht bei Leibniz und Hegel: Zur Interpretation der Klassengesellschaft* (Neuwied and Berlin: Luchterhand, 1968).

5

A Historical Comparison of Recognition
Attempt at a Systematic Summary

Within the three national cultures I have thus far examined, we find very different interpretations of the dependence of each subject on the recognition of its fellow humans. In early modern France, both La Rochefoucauld and Rousseau, as well as – much later – Sartre and Althusser, view this constitutive dependence primarily as a threat to our "authentic" relationship-to-self. In Great Britain, Shaftesbury, Hume, Smith and John Stuart Mill all view this dependence largely as a chance for moral self-control. Finally, around the turn of the nineteenth century in Germany, it is viewed by Kant, Fichte and Hegel as the condition of the possibility of individual self-determination. Before I turn to the difficult question of whether these starkly divergent connotations exclude or complement each other, whether they are mutually exclusive or combine to contribute to a more profound insight into the same phenomenon, I will attempt to summarize these differences in a more general manner, largely independently of these individual thinkers themselves. I will focus on the question of how precisely "recognition" is defined in these three different contexts as well as on the respective interpretations of its effect on the subjects involved, i.e. the recognizing and recognized individuals.

The first of these two questions poses significant difficulties, for recognition appears to refer to something different in each of the three different contexts. In the first, French context, recognition refers to a need to be esteemed or at least to attain a secured existence within society: partly to enjoy a position of social superiority, partly to be recognized as a legitimate member of the social community. It remains unclear whether this form of recognition is cognitive or normative, for often these subjects are described as merely desiring that others notice their own (presumed) characteristics, while in some instances they desire for these characteristics to be acknowledged as being morally exemplary. Which recognitional form is intended depends on the context, though in the tradition we have examined here, the epistemic connotation clearly outweighs the moral connotation. It thus also remains relatively unclear whether recognition has a gradual character, manifesting itself in different degrees. If the epistemic connotation outweighs the moral connotation, such gradation would seem impossible, because the "cognition" of "objective" facts can only be right or wrong; in the normative usage of the term, by contrast, varying degrees of recognition are certainly possible, as is illustrated by Rousseau's differentiation between equal respect and varied levels of esteem.

Matters are entirely different when it comes to the second context, that of primarily British thought. Although "recognition" here also refers to a natural human desire, the aim is not primarily to achieve a position of social superiority, but rather to achieve acceptance as a member of the social community. In this case recognition has a clearly normative meaning, as subjects expect to receive praise for their social behavior, for having sufficiently mastered the prevailing norms and demonstrating this through their actions. The gradual character of recognition in this tradition is enabled by the fact that the circle of individuals casting judgment on others' actions can constantly expand. The larger the group, the more reliable the guarantee of morally appropriate behavior. The third case of recognition, at home in German-speaking philosophy, is unique in that recognition here does not refer to a striving grounded in the nature of human desire, rather it represents a condition for becoming a rational, autonomous being. The reason for this universal dependence on the recognition of other humans is that we can only assure ourselves of our capacity to follow autonomous norms rather than empirical motives if we assure each other of this capacity. To recognize each other in this context means to refrain from realizing one's own desires, thus revealing our capacity for following norms we judge to be rational. It is not until Hegel comes along that this occurrence is stripped of its transcendental character and historicized, thus also enabling recognition to take on a gradual character: Hegel claims that there exist historically distinct forms of realizing mutual recognition, each of which raises the degree of human self-determination by demanding a higher degree of respect for others and reducing the possibility of asserting mere natural instincts.

These summarizing formulations are still too weighed down by the theories from which they originate to allow us to arrive at three clearly distinct paradigms of understanding our dependence on social recognition. Therefore, we must take the further step of distilling out three "ideal types" if we are to show sufficiently the contrasts between these different theories. It would probably not be wrong to claim that in the first paradigm, there is a tendency to conceive of the individual subject as a person whose desire for social recognition hopelessly exposes it to the judgment of society. Driven by the need for confirmation from the generalized other represented by all members of society, individuals will necessarily seek to act in accordance with socially established standards in order to receive admiration for their outstanding behavior; this desire is satisfied once an individual is recognized publicly for those characteristics for which it can also expect to receive the confirmation it desires. "Recognition" here refers to the social act of ascribing personal characteristics through which the subject can expect to find social acceptance and even admiration. Under the second paradigm, in which the individual is not conceived of as a slave to the judgment of society, but as a cooperative member in a social community, matters are different. The individual subject, driven by its desire for social acceptance, strives to morally control its behavior so as to receive social praise for following prevailing norms; this subject's need is satisfied as soon as the positive reaction of society demonstrates that it has been justifiably accepted as a member of the society of which it desires to be a part. "Recognition" in this case is a social act of moral praise that a subject must be able to imagine for itself in order to be confident of being respected as a legitimate member of the social community. In the third case, the subject is regarded neither as a slave to the judgment of society nor as a cooperative member of a social community. At the heart of this conception of recognition is a subject that struggles for autonomy within a social community. The individual actor, driven by its interest in realizing itself as a rational subject, depends on the reactions of others in order to discover whether it is capable of acting on reason alone. It is only capable of doing so if it refrains from asserting its own natural drives and shows others moral respect. "Recognition" therefore means a dyadic act of moral self-restriction that at least two subjects must perform in order to confirm each other's capacity for reason and thus each other's membership in a community of rational beings.

Obviously, these characterizations no longer bear any of the specific shadings that individual authors have given to the act of recognition. They do not take adequate account of the drastic differences between Rousseau's conception of "amour propre" and Sartre's theory of intersubjectivity, nor of the many distinctions between Hume's and Smith's versions of the inner spectator, nor of the grave differences between Fichte's transcendental concept of recognition and Hegel's historicized concept. To a certain degree that is just my intention, as the point is to distill the most general and shared features of recognition from all the culturally specific shadings in the characterization of our dependence on others, thus arriving at the three different current interpretations of recognition. Each of these "paradigms" contains one of the fundamental possibilities, i.e. independent of concrete experience, for imagining or conceiving of subjects' dependence on each other.

If we use this same approach to determine the effects of the various interpretations of recognition on the subjects involved, we will once again arrive at three very different conceptions. In the first paradigm, germane to French culture, recognition which ascribes personal characteristics has a negative, even destructive effect on the subject. An individual whose desire for social superiority or a socially secure existence is only satisfied when certain characteristics are publicly ascribed to it will lose the ability to determine or explore who it is and wants to be. In this tradition, therefore, intersubjective encounters are almost automatically associated with the threat of self-loss or self-alienation. This form of recognition entails the risk of no longer being capable of a first-person-perspective. Matters are much different when it comes to the effects of recognition under the second paradigm with its origins in Scottish moral philosophy. Here recognition is understood as moral praise or agreement, and its effect on the subject is generally described as being positive and socially beneficial. An individual whose desire for social membership can only be satisfied if its moral behavior and judgments are judged to be in line with the internalized norms of its community will feel compelled to subject its own social practices to constant moral inspection. In this tradition, therefore, intersubjective encounters are nearly automatically linked to the positive effect of learning to conform to the standards of the social community. The kind of recognition the subject receives from its "internal" observer, which in turn represents society as a whole, will reinforce its willingness to exercise moral self-control. Finally, there are the effects of recognition under the third paradigm, emerging from the practical philosophy of German Idealism. Here the distinction between the recognizing and the recognized subject vanishes in a certain sense; given the reciprocity of recognition assumed here, the subject must be capable of fulfilling both roles simultaneously. The effects of this form of mutual recognition, conceived of as a kind of normative authorization of our self- and co-determination, consists in both a restriction and an expansion of freedom at the same time. The individual whose need to realize its rationality can only be satisfied if it proves itself rational to its fellow humans will feel compelled to refrain from asserting its own merely egotistical interests, thus granting to others a measure of freedom that restricts its own freedom. And because its partners in interaction must likewise restrict their own freedom in order to demonstrate that they, too, are rational beings, they will in turn grant the recognizing subject a normative status that increases the latter's own freedom. In the third tradition, therefore, mutual recognition is interpreted as the condition of the possibility of individual self-determination. The recognition that individuals grant each other in order to prove their own rational subjectivity enables them to exercise their freedom in a socially acceptable manner.

This attempt to summarize these three theories of recognition in a way that reveals three "ideal types" of recognition demonstrates just how far apart the conceptions of intersubjective encounters developed in the cultures of France, Great Britain and Germany are. The profound differences between these three culturally specific paradigms relate not only to the expectations and attitudes at work in these encounters, but also to the effects of these encounters on the subjects involved. In the French context, the individual striving for social status or a secure social existence results in the danger of self-loss, while in the British context, the individual need for social approval generates the willingness for moral self-control; and finally, in the German-speaking context, the demand that we mutually recognize each other enables the possibility of individual self-determination. These significantly different conceptions of intersubjective encounters raise the question of how we should conceive of the relationship between them. Do they merely cast one and the same phenomenon – the intersubjective relation of recognition – in a different light, or do they reveal complementary aspects that, taken together, produce a more complex understanding of intersubjective encounters? The same question could be posed differently by focusing on the consequences of these reconstructed traditions for current debates on the idea of recognition. I want to approach this difficult issue by sweeping aside a few misunderstandings in current discussions of the issue in order to explore possibilities for mediating between these three different models.

Given these major differences – in terms of both theoretical approach and result – which I have attempted to sort among three "ideal types" of recognition, it might seem possible simply to claim that these three models of recognition are irreconcilable. Yet, contrary to the currently dominant notion that the field of recognition theory is occupied by a "positive" and a "negative" approach, both of which operate on the same level and merely provide contrasting accentuations,[1] we must

---

[1] See Rahel Jaeggi and Ronin Celikates, *Sozialphilosophie: Eine Einführung* (Munich: Beck, 2017), ch. 5, esp. pp. 69ff. The key texts in this "negative" tradition, alongside the works of Jean-Paul Sartre, Louis Althusser and Judith Butler (between which there are grave differences), include Patchen Markell, *Bound by Recognition* (Princeton: Princeton University

first emphasize the seemingly insurmountable difficulties of comparing these theories to each other. What is termed "recognition" in the so-called "positive" tradition of Fichte and Hegel is so different from the "negative" tradition typically associated with Louis Althusser or Judith Butler (thus also neglecting the intellectual inheritance of Rousseau and Sartre) that we can hardly treat recognition as one and the same phenomenon. On the one hand, the term refers merely to the social ascription of certain (typifying) properties without any normative component of "self-restriction" on the part of the ascribing subject, while on the other hand the same term refers to the moral authorization that necessarily goes along with a commitment to restrict one's own actions. For Fichte, Hegel and the members of the tradition they founded, recognition is (a profoundly Kantian thought) a stance and a way of acting toward other subjects, which enables the latter (perhaps to different degrees) to act in a self-determined way, to perform acts of their "free will" by (again, perhaps to various degrees) refraining from following their "own self-love" (Kant), thus acting in a purely self-referential manner. If an attitude or mode of action does not possess this second element of moral self-restriction on the part of the recognizing subject, then it cannot be called "recognition" in the Fichtean and Hegelian tradition; rather, we would have to refer to such attitudes and actions as social "ascription" or "classification". This profound distinction is not changed by the fact that the so-called negative tradition associated with French thought is also claimed to regard the

Press, 2003); Thomas Bedorf, *Verkennende Anerkennung: Über Identität und Politik* (Berlin: Suhrkamp, 2010).

social production of a "free will" or a self-conscious subject as the result of "recognition". In both traditions, the same formulation refers to very different things. In the one instance, it refers to the socially guaranteed enabling of self-determination; in the other, it refers to the fiction of a self-determination undermined by socially imposed determinations.[2]

Just as fatal as conflating these two concepts that stem from different traditions is neglecting the notion of recognition that stems from Scottish moral philosophy. If I am not mistaken, this idea of recognition has come to define our everyday use of the term more than the two other theoretical paradigms. The understanding of "recognition" as the social distinction or esteem granted to a person's good behavior, which through constant repetition is then internalized as a psychological authority over one's behavior, is found at the core of popular psychology and has left its trace in contemporary moral philosophy as well. According to the latter, and implicitly picking up on the empiricist tradition, "praise" and "shame" represent public means for securing the validity of moral norms in society.[3] Given the widespread use of the term, it is all the more astounding that this everyday conception of the social

---

[2] See, e.g., Althusser, *Ideology and Ideological State Apparatuses*, p. 263. Judith Butler is even more explicit in her book *The Psychic Life of Power*, p. 9.

[3] See the use of recognition in this context in Peter Stemmer, *Normativität: Eine ontologische Untersuchung* (Berlin: de Gruyter, 2008). Just how muddled the use of the term "recognition" has become in contemporary moral philosophy is made clear by the fact that David Wiggins manages to found his conception of an ethics – picking up on Hume and Philippa Foot – in the "mutual recognition" characteristic of our form of life without even mentioning the origin of this idea in the works of Fichte and

value of interpersonal confirmation and approval plays almost no role at all in current debates on the meaning and effects of social recognition. We hardly ever hear of the fact that such elementary, everyday techniques of recognitional encouragement are used to educate young children, to teach adolescents to develop a strong sense of self and to function among adults as a means of mutual motivation to pursue ambitious goals. Once again, however, we must note that in these cases the term "recognition" indicates an entirely different social act from the other two uses of the term. Unlike the "negative" approach and in line with the conceptions of recognition stemming from German Idealism, this understanding of recognition emphasizes the normative aspect of agreement while lacking the additional component of simultaneous moral self-restriction. Praise and distinction are recognitional reactions, but they do not require that we restrict our own self-referentiality at the same time – a crucial element of the concept of recognition rooted in Kant's idea of respect. The current discussion is thus thematically one-sided and ignores conceptual differences, presenting a great jumble of intuitions of various origins, and so making it entirely unclear how they could ever form a whole.

How might the three divergent models of recognition be linked so as to make them no longer mutually exclusive, but productively complementary? In other words, is there a way to read these different conceptions, each deriving from culturally specific experiences, as historically gained insights into divergent aspects or forms of realizing one and the same process?

Hegel: David Wiggins, *Ethics: Twelve Lectures on the Philosophy of Morality* (Cambridge, MA: Harvard University Press, 2006), pp. 243ff.

This would mean interpreting them as contributing to a more complex understanding of what it means for us humans to be dependent on others' recognition. In the conclusion of my historical study I would at least like to provide a sketch of how these three models of recognition could in fact be integrated – thus guarding against the impression that I am merely resigning myself to the finding that Europe is home to very different ways of philosophically understanding our dependence on others due to the existence of different individual countries and cultures and preventing us from drawing any systematic conclusions. It is one thing to take note of the various paths of development an idea has taken historically, and another thing entirely to undertake a systematic inquiry into their respective justifications.

For my purposes, however, it will occasionally be advisable to partially qualify my own attempt to generalize the three culturally specific traditions and fashion them into comprehensive "paradigms". We will see that some approaches in the traditions of thought I have dealt with here can be more easily integrated into a coherent understanding of our dependence on social recognition. For example, right away we will see that Sartre's ontological analysis of the necessary transformation of every experience of recognition into a state of reified obligation is hardly reconcilable with positive assessments of the effects of being addressed by another person. In this case, the odd and oft-criticized presuppositions in Sartre's concept of human subjectivity are what make it impossible to bring his approach into line with other ways of describing the act of recognition.[4] The example of Sartre shows just how difficult it

---

[4] See pp. 45–46 in this book.

is to theoretically integrate our three different ideas of recognition; we are dealing not only with merely apparent irreconcilabilities with regard to the essence and effects of recognition, but also with starkly contrasting methodological approaches. At first sight it seems impossible to combine approaches that employ such divergent forms of justification: psychological-phenomenological descriptions, conclusions from generally perceptible experiences, transcendental analyses or historical-philosophical lines of argumentation. I do believe, however, that we could find a solution to this problem by first of all abstracting from such methodological differences and asking which of the three models makes the strongest claim in terms of explaining our social form of life as a whole. On the basis of the most fundamental, constitutive understanding of recognition, we could then ask what we would have to change, correct or supplement in the image of our social life in order to integrate the other two models of recognition. If such a procedure, which admittedly seems arbitrary at first glance, allows us to gain a more complex understanding of our mutual dependence on social recognition, then it will be possible for all three of these models to be integrated in a fruitful way. It is only in retrospect, however, that we will be able to determine whether this approach can in fact bridge the methodological differences between the various approaches, or at least minimize them to a degree that they no longer stand in the way of theoretical integration. We cannot ignore the fact that the difficulty in combining these three models derives not only from conceptually different meanings of recognition, but also from crucial distinctions in the underlying method of cognition.

Given my historical observations, it should come as no surprise that I propose making the understanding of recognition stemming from the tradition of German Idealism the foundation for integrating all three models of recognition. The reasons for this choice will become apparent once we attempt to clarify what it was that Fichte and Hegel sought to explain with their respective conceptions of recognition at the most general level. In spite of all the differences between them, both thinkers sought to make plausible what it means for humans to live in a "spiritual world" primarily characterized by our orientation toward shared norms. This necessarily entails mutually ascribing – as a role or normative status – the authority to co-determine what norms are appropriate and how they should be implemented.[5] Hegel and Fichte thus claim that we can only comprehend the social interaction of human subjects by assuming that they reciprocally recognize each other as beings with the authority to decide for themselves whether their shared and practiced norms merit approval. This understanding of recognition, an intersubjectivist reinterpretation of Kant's notion of respect, can be considered more fundamental than the other two understandings of recognition, for it describes the communicative conditions under which social recognition can take place at all. Regardless of whether I perceive the other as an authority to whose judgment I submit, as is the case in

---

[5] See Heikki Ikäheimo's notion of "deontological Neo-Hegelianism" in *Anerkennung*, pp. 168–71. See also Titus Stahl, *Immanente Kritik: Elemente einer Theorie sozialer Praktiken* (Frankfurt: Campus, 2013), ch. 4.7.

the British tradition, or whether I view the other as an authority whose evaluation of my behavior I desperately seek, as is
the case in the Rousseauian tradition, both cases presuppose
the recognition of the other as a person who is authorized to
co-determine our common life. In this sense, therefore, the
idea of recognition proposed by Fichte and Hegel, whose
fundamental insight can be found in various versions
today,[6] can be regarded as the foundation of the other two
models of recognition. The model which Fichte and Hegel
describe either negatively or positively presupposes that subjects have already reciprocally recognized each other as co-
authors of the norms they share.

Yet, as we have already seen, Hegel was not content
with the merely "transcendental" finding that this reciprocal
ascription of normative authority is constitutive for human
moral life. On the basis of his proposal that we view the
"spiritual world" as a historically unfolding structure that
only gradually reveals its inner potential, he felt justified in
assuming a sequence of institutionally concretized relations of
recognition based on various different norms. The social
practices in which we commit to shared social norms by

---

[6] Alongside the already mentioned notion of "deontological Neo-
Hegelianism", see the works of Karl-Otto Apel (see above, ch. 4, n. 37,
p. 96) and Jürgen Habermas (see e.g. "From Kant to Hegel and Back
Again: The Move toward Detranscendentalization", in *Truth and
Justification* (Cambridge, MA: MIT Press, 2003), pp. 175–211). See also
Stephen Darwall, *The Second-Person Standpoint: Morality, Respect and
Accountability* (Cambridge, MA: Harvard University Press, 2009),
although Darwall does not draw any connections to the tradition of
Fichte and Hegel.

granting each other the right to examine and interpret our actions thereby lose their ahistorical invariance; instead they take on several forms distinguishable from each other in terms of the possibilities they make available to us.[7] For my purposes we need not concern ourselves for the moment with the fact that Hegel understood these distinctions between various forms of recognition in a normative fashion: the freer the subjects are to examine the appropriateness and the implementation of their shared norms, the more advanced the given structure of recognition will be. Here we need only note that Hegel's historicizing of the "spiritual world" gives empirical shape to the grounded practices of reciprocal recognition, which makes its difference from the other concepts of recognition seem much less significant. Although Hegel, like Fichte, locates the motive for such practices in the desire of individuals to realize their free subjectivity, he must detranscendentalize these practices and imbue

---

[7] Were we find very close parallels to what Jürgen Habermas terms "relations of communication" or "relations of understanding", which are also conceived of as being capable of changing over time and increasing in rationality. On the significance of this key idea in the work of Habermas, see Dieter Henrich, "Kritik der Verständigungsverhältnisse", in Henrich and Habermas, *Zwei Reden: Aus Anlaß des Hegel-Preises* (Frankfurt: Suhrkamp, 1974), pp. 9–22. This is incidentally the one point on which I disagree with Heikki Ikäheimo's excellent introduction to the topic of recognition (see his *Anerkennung*), because he claims that different forms of recognition represent independent types of recognition corresponding to distinct moral challenges in our form of life (ch. 7.2). By contrast I agree with Hegel that these different forms derive from a differentiation of a single occurrence of the mutual ascription of a "normative status", through which the type of permissible reasons and the extent of the relevant segments of personality are also transformed.

them with enough concrete experience to give them the character of real occurrences in the life-world, just as is true of the British and French tradition. With respect to Hegel's understanding of social recognition – unlike that of Fichte – we can reasonably pose the question whether and to what extent the other two models of recognition supplement or correct his theory. If the mutuality of recognition only took place in spiritual space, without any anchoring in the reality of social practices and institutions, then the psychological or empirical observations of Rousseau, Hume and Smith could hardly make any contribution to a more profound analysis.

It cannot, in my opinion, be too difficult to draw a connection between Hegel's theory of recognition and the British conception of an "inner spectator". To be able to do so, we first need to recall what Hegel sought to explain by means of the concept of recognition. He intended to clarify what it means for humans to live in a "spiritual world", i.e. in a world not determined merely by the laws of nature. Like Kant and Fichte, Hegel assumes that this entails that our thought and our actions are not determined by natural drives but by self-determined norms. Unlike Kant, and in agreement with Fichte, Hegel did not regard this act of self-determination as an individual act of submission to a pre-existing and eternally unchanging ethical law, but as a cooperative endeavor through which we produce such norms by conceding each other the authority to judge the appropriateness of our norms and the implementation of our imperatives and rules.[8] That

---

[8] Robert B. Brandom is wonderfully clear on this point: "Recollections of Idealism" (draft available online), ch. 2.4.

which constitutes societies as "spiritual worlds", therefore, is a practice in which subjects mutually recognize each other as co-authors of their shared norms. Unlike Fichte, however, Hegel was convinced that such practices do not initially exist in the form demanded by their "concept" [*Begriff*]. In order to ensure social conditions under which all subjects can recognize each other as equal normative authorities, he felt a long historical process would have to take place in which an institutionally concretized, yet still insufficient, order of recognition would gradually be replaced by an order that would better correspond to its "concept", and would thus be more free and just. As I have attempted to show, Hegel thereby not only sought to prove that social norms are predicated on the reciprocity of normative authorization, which thereby constitutes a precondition for all social life; rather, by historicizing this basic relation of recognition, he also sought to create the possibility of regarding this relation as a set of practices rooted in the life-world and structured by institutions – practices engaged in by living subjects driven by moral concerns. In spite of the astounding proximity of Hegel's account to social reality, however, it remains unclear just how we are to conceive of the fact that these socially situated subjects follow their cooperatively created and practiced norms in almost automatic conformity. It is precisely at this point, at which we seek to explain the transformation of cooperatively shaped norms into the harmony of social customs, that the understanding of recognition in Scottish moral philosophy takes on a function that supplements Hegel's theory.

In order to explain why the members of society follow their commonly "managed" norms largely in motivational harmony, Hegel draws on Aristotle's concept of *habitus*, which the latter develops in the context of his ethical theory. According to this theory, we develop a "good character" by undergoing an educational process in which we repeatedly imitate virtuous behavior and thus become so accustomed to finding pleasure at the right moments that we ultimately develop a permanent disposition for ethically appropriate behavior.[9] Yet regardless of how fruitful this concept might have proven to be and how productive its influence might have been on the discipline of sociology,[10] it leaves us in the dark concerning both the psychological process of moral habituation and the initial motive for this process. Hegel himself, who appropriated Aristotle's notion for his belief that our moral customs represent a kind of second nature,[11] has little to say about how we actually learn and internalize social norms. In my view, matters would have been different if Hegel had not solely followed Aristotle's theoretical lead, but picked up on the insights of the Scottish enlightenment as well. If Hegel had taken the trouble to consider Hume and Smith's thoughts on the formation of moral habits, this would have had two great advantages. He would have had an easier time uncovering both the motives and the psychological

[9] Aristotle, *Nicomachean Ethics* (Cambridge: Cambridge University Press, 2000), Book II (pp. 23–35).
[10] On the revival of the idea of habitus in sociology, see Pierre Bourdieu, *Outline of a Theory of Practice* (Cambridge: Cambridge University Press, 1977), pp. 78–86.
[11] See Axel Honneth, "Zweite Natur – Untiefen eines philosophischen Schlüsselbegriffs", in Julia Christ and Axel Honneth, eds, *Zweite Natur: Internationaler Hegelkongress 2017* (to be published).

process by which individuals learn to internalize commonly established norms. With respect to the motives for internalizing such norms, Hegel shared Fichte's standard view that the desire to assert oneself as a rational being is what moves individuals to commit to norms found to be generally reasonable. However, in view of the concrete historical shape Hegel sought to give to his theory of recognition, this solution does not suffice, because it does not tell us enough about the actually effective motives at work here. Hegel thus should have followed Adam Smith, if not David Hume as well, in viewing the striving for membership in the social community as the decisive motive for the individual willingness to follow social norms. Hegel could have easily grasped this desire or need as the life-world aspect of his "spiritual" drive to realize one's own rationality. In this case, individuals would be motivated to adopt the moral norms of their social community in their everyday life by the subjective expectation of receiving the approval of the other members of society, thus allowing them to regard themselves as members of the same community.

An even more important point concerns the process by which we adopt social norms. While the psychological aspects of this process remain relatively obscure in the Aristotelian notion of habitus (here we find a rather mechanistic conception in which external impulses are translated into physical automatisms), Hume and Smith's idea of an "inner spectator" offers a much more complex explanation, according to which we should conceive of the motivational adoption of moral norms as a process by which we learn to reproduce the expectations of our social environment until these expectations manage to control our behavior as the voice of our own conscience. Certainly the term "inner spectator" or "judge" has an unfortunately metaphorical touch, encouraging us to imagine something like a person within a person; at the same time, however, the notion is capable of building a conceptual bridge from the social considerations of Sigmund Freud, who interpreted the formation of the moral superego as the impression that the positive reactions of parents on the behavior of the child makes on the latter's psychological apparatus. Here, just as in the case of Adam Smith, the recognition of our loved ones continues to function as an inner voice, constantly reminding adults of their moral duties.[12] We do not need Freud's help, however, to prove the significance of Smith's theory for explaining how we form moral habits. Not only does Smith's theory stand on its own two feet, but its interpretive power is likely even superior to that of Freud, for it accounts for the possibility of a successive generalization of this inner authority until all personal preferences are nearly eliminated. In any case, these few allusions to the *Theory of Moral Sentiments* should suffice to justify the proposal that we view the British theory of recognition as a useful supplement to Hegel's view of mutual recognition. The idea of an "inner spectator" is superior to Hegel when it comes to explaining how subjects that

---

[12] At least this is one of the versions of Freud's account of the origins of the conscience or super-ego. See Sigmund Freud, *Civilization and Its Discontents* (New York: Norton, 1961), p. 124: "This state of mind is called a 'bad conscience', but actually it does not deserve this name, for at this stage the sense of guilt is clearly only a fear of loss of love, 'social anxiety'."

recognize each other's moral authority manage to transform their commonly established and confirmed norms into everyday habits. This is made possible, according to Smith, by a gradual shift of perspective from the second person to one's own self, such that the former monitors my behavior in the form of my conscience, examining whether my actions are reconcilable with the social expectations of a continuously growing community. Although Hegel certainly does have a notion of personal "conscience", he grasps it as a mere representative of the Kantian universalist moral principles of which he is so skeptical,[13] and not as the psychological representation of the moral reactions of a gradually "generalized" other. The gap between abstract morality and ethical convictions that thus arises in Hegel's practical philosophy is something Hegel can only manage to bridge by positing the formation of ethics or ethical habits as a transformational process in which external expectations of behavior become relatively stable automatisms. If Hegel, as I have sketched here, had instead supplemented his basic theory of recognition with Smith's model of socialization, he would have been spared such a fragmented solution. The conscience of the individual, which is grasped in a more flexible and plural way than in the work of Kant, i.e. as a concert of many voices representing the moral reactions of various groups and institutional circles in our own psyche, would always ensure that

---

[13] This is why Hegel, too, discusses the issue of conscience in the section of his *Philosophy of Right* on "morality": G. W. F. Hegel, *Elements of the Philosophy of Right* (Cambridge: Cambridge University Press, 1991), §136 (pp. 163f.).

commonly authorized norms do in fact have a practical effect on us.

Such a solution, which I have only briefly sketched here, does of course presuppose that we conceive of the highly disparate understandings of recognition in German Idealism and the empiricist tradition of Great Britain as being somehow reconcilable. According to the conception I have outlined, the relation between these two understandings is that Hegel's notion defines the elementary conditions of mutual recognition under which a constantly changing life-world can be regarded as being normatively regulated at all, whereas Hume and Smith's conception names the practices of social approval and affirmation by which cooperatively constructed norms become anchored in individuals' own systems of motivation. In the first case, the term "recognition" indicates the practice of mutual authorization to create and examine norms; in the second case, it merely refers to the affirmative reaction of an already normatively constituted community to the moral behavior of individual members of society. The gap between these two uses of the term "recognition" is huge, but the fact that they have both managed to have such an influence on our everyday use of the term should be reason enough to account for the relation between them.

Certainly the same cannot be said for the French conception of the value and effects of intersubjective recognition. We can hardly claim that there is any negative connotation to our everyday conception of what it means to be socially recognized, contrary to the claims made by Rousseau, Sartre and Althusser. There are, as we have seen, peculiar sociocultural causes for this fact, deriving in my view from the major significance of symbolic distinction in French social life, which is in turn due in great part to the extremely centralized nature of the country. Still, we must also examine whether such a negative understanding of recognition might also emphasize an aspect of recognition that merits integration into the framework of Hegel's theory. When it comes to the French tradition, we are faced with far greater difficulties than in the case of the British tradition, for as soon as we remove the artificial glue provided by the models that bind these different approaches, we see entirely different intuitions at work. We would certainly not be wrong in claiming that the kind of social perception underlying Rousseau's negative conception of recognition differs greatly from the critical observations found in Butler's or Althusser's conception of social recognition. Although I have included both concepts in one and the same tradition, given that both reinterpret recognition as an act of ascription and emphasize the negative effects of recognition on an individual's relation-to-self, I will now put stronger emphasis on the differences in their respective relations to Hegel's basic understanding of recognition. I will begin with the intuition underlying Rousseau's negative conception and then turn to the ideas of Judith Butler and Louis Althusser.

Rousseau's negative understanding of recognition had its point of departure in the observation that "amour propre" awakens within humans a poisonous striving for superiority in the eyes of their partners in interaction. In order to be able to analyze this desire more closely, the Genevan philosopher reinterpreted the "inner judge", familiar to him from the works of Hume, as a strict observer whose gaze compels its fellow humans to do everything to appear to possess personal characteristics justifying their social position. "Recognition" in the eyes of Rousseau, therefore, is the ascription of attributes that serve to improve one's own reputation in society. Rousseau was also convinced that this masquerade would cause the subject to struggle to understand at all who he or she is in her true nature or inner essence. This is why I propose that we interpret Rousseau as the founder of the idea, largely found in France, that individual self-loss represents the flipside or stepson of all social recognition. However, as I pointed out in connection with *Émile* and the *Social Contract*,[14] there are a number of places in the work of Rousseau that suggest a less negative reading of his theory of recognition. For instance, he mentions that "amour propre" can also be satisfied in the healthy and socially beneficial manner of equal, mutual respect; here it suddenly seems as if the boasting and bragging described in the Second Discourse merely represent pathological, out-of-control forms of a harmless desire for social acceptance and validity. The more we emphasize this interpretation of Rousseau's theory of recognition and thereby bracket the fact that his later works then move back in the other direction, the easier it will be to draw a highly fruitful connection to Hegel's theory. The author of *Philosophy of Right*, too, is familiar with pathological forms of mutual recognition; and just like his French predecessor, he believes they are caused by social phenomena such as affectedness and a craving for recognition. Yet, in order to understand at just what point these two theories

[14] See above, pp. 28–30.

intertwine and supplement each other, we must give a somewhat more detailed account of Hegel's argument than I have provided thus far.

As I have already pointed out, Hegel did not want the mutuality of normative authorization to be understood as a merely mental occurrence in a vacuum, but as a historical and gradually unfolding practice engaged in by living individuals. He thus sought to identify the institutional relations in which this practice had already taken hold, depending on the stage in the realization of its own concept. Hegel, however, carried out such a "normative reconstruction"[15] of constantly changing forms of recognition only for his own time, early modernity. The result of his efforts is the *Philosophy of Right*, in which he identifies the modern family, the capitalist market and the constitutional monarchy as the three institutional spheres in which subjects authorize each other in different roles respectively to examine the norms they put into practice, thus confirming their own autonomy anchored in the lifeworld. Directly relevant for my question is primarily the fact that Hegel continuously casts his gaze on the psychological phenomena that seemed to be caused by the exclusion of certain individuals or groups from institutionalized practices of mutual recognition. Examples of such occurrences are "the renunciation of shame and honor" on the part of the long-term unemployed among the "rabble",[16] as well as the

---

[15] On my proposal that we follow Hegel's own usage of the terms "descriptive" or "observing" to capture this procedure, see Axel Honneth, *The Right of Freedom: The Social Foundations of Democratic Life* (New York: Columbia University Press, 2015).

[16] Hegel, *Philosophy of Right*, §245 (p. 267).

tendency for merely "external manifestations" of one's own professional skills among the "professional" classes [*Gewerbetreibenden*] who are not capable of becoming members of a "corporation" [*Korporation*].[17] Hegel regards such psychological phenomena as more than just incidental, rather as socially produced pathologies that necessarily emerge once members of society are not sufficiently included in the institutional sphere of mutual recognition. This is not only a striking indication of how much Hegel, unlike Fichte, grasped the subjects or bearers of such processes of recognition as human beings of flesh and blood; separations between physical bodies, the psyche and the mind are entirely alien to him. What is most important for our purposes is that these remarks prove how much Hegel sought to combine his analyses of the institutional reality of social processes of recognition with psychological observations that bear an astounding resemblance to those of Rousseau.

The second pathology Hegel names – that of the members of "professional classes" not organized in "corporations" – shows a striking proximity between Hegel and Rousseau. The formulations Hegel employs to describe the psychological reactions of those excluded from the recognition taking place within "corporations" all sound as if they had been directly borrowed from Rousseau's Second Discourse. He writes that the members of society are forced to revert to the "egotistical side" of their trade, having no choice but to show their "honor" through pretentious displays of their skills. In short, in Rousseau's terms, they are driven by an "impudent" inclination for boasting

[17] Ibid., §253 (pp. 271f.).

and bragging. If we summarize these characterizations, we could claim that Hegel interpreted the hypostasized, out-of-control forms of "amour propre" in the work of Rousseau as the result of psychological compensation for withheld recognition. He seems convinced that those who remain excluded from institutionalized relations of recognition, and thus cannot experience themselves as having normative authority within the framework of these relations, will necessarily develop certain behavioral disorders almost identical to those found in the Second Discourse. If this interpretation is correct, that is, if Hegel understands the "inflamed" (Neuhouser) forms of "amour propre" as symptoms of efforts at compensation, then we will have found a bridge between these two thinkers' theories of recognition. In this case, both the German and the French philosopher will have viewed selfishness, vanity and a craving for recognition as reactions to the experience of being excluded from a community founded on mutual recognition or equal respect. Despite the possibility of interweaving these two authors' theories of recognition, the fact remains, however, that we are dealing with two very different terminologies whose differences we cannot forget. Rousseau viewed "amour propre" exclusively as an empirical human desire to achieve status within society – and this would still be the case if he had sought to distinguish between healthy and unhealthy, socially acceptable and socially harmful forms of this desire. For Hegel, by contrast, the "need" for social recognition was "spiritually" motivated, stemming from humans' drive to realize themselves as rational beings, which Hegel occasionally translated into the life-world motivation to be part of a society of subjects who follow norms. Correspondingly large are the differences between these two thinkers' concepts of recognition. Rousseau interpreted that which the empirical desire for "amour propre" seeks to satisfy as a kind of social ascription of qualities – be they qualities shared by all humans or those by which we distinguish ourselves from others and which enable us to feel superior to them. For Hegel, on the other hand, the social reaction capable of satisfying our desire to be regarded as rational subjects had to consist in an act of recognition that gives us the right to cooperate in the shared process of establishing norms, thus restricting the freedom of other participants in this process. Nevertheless, despite the major differences in terms of their systematic premises, there is one point in the diagnosis of social pathologies at which the conceptions of Rousseau and Hegel meet. Both seem to share the idea that humans generally tend to respond to the withholding of equal respect or reciprocal recognition with pretentious behavior and the vain display of supposed merits. At this point, where the psychology of social recognition is involved, Hegel's theory can be supplemented by Rousseau's insights.

The question, however, is whether the same could be shown to be true of the branch of the French tradition culminating in the works of Althusser. The intuition from which this second variety of a negative understanding of recognition derives differs significantly from that of Rousseau, even though both ultimately agree on the diagnosis of a threat of self-loss, which, for Rousseau, consists in an altered personality and, for Althusser (and Butler), consists in a kind of social recognition that merely stabilizes relations of domination. In my discussion of this second offspring of typically French negativism, we already saw just how deep the chasm is between this concept of recognition and that of Hegel and Fichte. In the first case, "recognition" hardly means more than a type of respect that subjects show by authorizing each other to examine and interpret commonly practiced norms. The difference could thus hardly be any greater between these two usages of the concept of recognition. So where in the use of the concept lies the spark that might be capable of setting off a rethinking within the tradition Hegel established so solidly?

A hint at where such a spark might lie can in fact be found in Hegel's *Philosophy of Right* itself. In a passage concerning the "family", often commented upon in recent years, Hegel wrote that the wife has the "determination" or role of providing "an emotive and subjective ethical life", which is why she must submit to her husband and find her place in the "home" [*Hauswesen*].[18] Even worse, and in the same context, he goes on to say that the woman, given her incapacity for "universality" and "the ideal", resembles a "plant", while the man, due to his "work and struggle with the external world" is comparable to "animal".[19] Especially puzzling about such formulations is less the horrendous degree of misogyny, obvious to us today, but rather the fact that Hegel, just a few lines later, resolutely claims that men "should not count more than women", and that in modern marriage, both are "equal, with the same rights and duties" [*Dieselbigkeit der Rechte und der Pflichten*].[20] Hegel, therefore, appears to see no contradiction

---

[18] G. W. F. Hegel, *Grundlinien der Philosophie des Rechts* (Frankfurt: Suhrkamp, 1986), §167, Anmerkung (p. 320).

[19] Hegel, *Philosophy of Right*, §166 (p. 206).

[20] Hegel, *Grundlinien*, §167, Anmerkung (p. 321).

between the presupposed submission of the woman to the man within marriage and a relationship to her husband on the basis of mutual recognition. As if there was no friction between these two standpoints, Hegel describes this relation as an institutionalized sphere of recognition in which man and woman mutually respect each other's autonomy – while the woman still gets the short end of the stick, as she is subordinated to the directives of her husband. This obvious dissonance in Hegel's argumentation can only be resolved if we can explain why he believes that women, on the basis of the normative authority granted to them, should agree to their own subordination. It is this very point that I believe Althusser's understanding of recognition, which could not seem more alien to Hegel's, can nevertheless serve to expand and consummate Hegel's theory.

In order to get a better sense of this possibility, we first require a more precise description of the relation of recognition Hegel sees between man and woman in modern marriage, which is no longer based on parental arrangements but "affection" [*Zuneigung*]. The norm whose implementation both partners can examine and question – due to the mutual authorization they grant each other through recognition – is that of "mutual love and support",[21] as well as the "satisfaction of the natural drive", i.e. sexual needs, even if the latter are ethically restricted.[22] Given what we already know about Hegel's viewpoint, this means that man and woman in marriage are equally entitled to question the way the respective other puts this norm into practice, and to propose new

[21] *Philosophy of Right*, §164 (p. 204).
[22] Ibid., §163 (pp. 202f., esp. Addition).

forms for doing so. They may thereby make reference to any reasons that can be regarded as legitimate within the horizon of their shared norms. In the case of "mutual love and support", therefore, they can invoke subjective desires, emotions and overarching life-aims. In Hegel's view, the rules and procedures involved in such a relation of recognition are variable because they can always be called into question; and this form of recognition seems fundamentally to exclude the possibility that the wife, discontented with her merely subordinate role, could ever object to such norms. The idea that she does not and will not do so anytime soon must be due to something outside of the norm and the possibilities of its interpretation – something that restricts the understanding and interpretation of this norm so fundamentally that there seems to be no possibility of the woman actually objecting to it anytime in the future. This "outside" is for Hegel, as we have already seen, "nature" itself. Entirely contrary to his general belief that the history of recognition is one of constant overcoming of and emancipation from the determinations of nature, at this point in the system modern married life, an element of completely unmediated nature, suddenly intrudes into the most developed relation of recognition. Hegel is convinced that now and in the future women will assent to an interpretation of marriage that completely subordinates them to their husbands, because they will regard this as their natural female vocation. Hegel thus smuggles a natural determination into his construction of marriage – one that we now know to be a mere appearance, but not an irreversible hard fact. Some of the reasons and normative arguments women justifiably employ with regard to their position in marriage do not even occur to Hegel, for in his eyes they would violate the nature of gender relations and thus be completely invalid as moral reasons.

What is remarkable about this small detail of Hegel's philosophy of right is certainly not the fact that it reveals just how conservative and even reactionary Hegel's thought on marriage and the family was. Hegel shared with most, if not all of his contemporaries the notion that women, given their natural predisposition, belong in the home and not in the public sphere of employed labor and politics. What is remarkable for our purposes is the fact that the mutual authorization to examine the implementation of shared norms does not tell us anything about the reasons at the disposal of those involved. What can be presented as a legitimate reason in such a relation of recognition is obviously not determined by what the participants believe can and cannot be changed, what is social construct and what is natural. The size of the space of the reasons upon which objections to the prevailing interpretation of a shared norm can be based within a given order of recognition is not determined solely by the fact that the participants mutually grant each other the equal right to judge and criticize their shared practices. What determines the number of legitimate reasons that can be brought forth, and thus what can be criticized, objected to or called into question, are instead worldviews and systems of interpretation that intrude into the relation of recognition from the outside by distinguishing between the unchangeable and the changeable, between nature and culture. The greater the space taken up in such a relation of recognition by what the participants view as natural and thus unchangeable on the basis of such distinctions that are made behind their backs, so to say, the less space there is for reasons they can act on. Therefore, as the example of Hegel's view on marriage shows, every order of recognition must be examined in terms of whether something is falsely experienced as nature which in fact must be viewed as culture. If such a proof has been carried out and adopted by at least some of the participants, the space of reasons available for use in such examinations will immediately expand.

It is this blind spot in Hegel's theory of recognition that, in my view, can be eliminated by employing the arsenal offered by Althusser's theory of recognition. After all, the point is to explain why individuals must eventually come to view personal characteristics they either only accidentally or do not possess at all as naturally given, unchangeable and thus unquestionable. Such a "naturalization" of contingent behavioral aspects should not, however, be conceived of in the form in which they have taken effect historically: as a justification for excluding entire social collectives from relations of recognition that are constitutive for society. Hegel is of course also familiar with such cases, for example that of slaves, but also that of women, who among some "peoples" enjoy "little respect".[23] However, neither of these is relevant to those cases in which the equality present in historically advanced relations of recognition is undermined – the very cases that need to be explained here. If we take into account this distinction and grasp the Althusserian theory of recognition as referring primarily to the second case, in which naturalized characteristics restrict the space of potential

---

[23] Ibid., §162, Addition (p. 202).

reasons in a relationship of reciprocal recognition, then the explanation offered by Althusser and his successors could be described as follows. Because members of one and the same circle of individuals are repeatedly and almost ritually "summoned" with the same, highly type-specific characteristics – in school, in encounters with the bureaucracy, in church or in the workplace – they will develop a tendency to grasp the characteristics ascribed to them as fixed elements of their own nature. Within the relations of reciprocal recognition described by Hegel, the appearance of fixed, natural behavioral dispositions – a product of the recognition organized or mediated by the state – has the effect of excluding a sector from the pool of possible reasons for accepting or rejecting a previously established practice, for it seems to violate the nature of the individuals involved. Such a relationship of recognition, though intended to prevent relations of domination, would in fact perpetuate that relation of subordination by intervening from above in a type of recognition that compels the participants to perceive themselves as possessing characteristics they necessarily view as being unchangeable elements of their own nature.

However, this attempt to draw a loose connection between Hegel's and Althusser's theory of recognition surely appears somewhat artificial; after all, we hardly even need the concept of recognition to make this connection. We could describe the same processes that Althusser and Judith Butler have in mind with the use of entirely different and perhaps even more appropriate conceptual tools. For instance, we could grasp the individual self-assignment to a group defined by "natural" features such as "gender" or "race" as the looping effect of a politically defined and relatively stable classification.[24] Or we could, in starker opposition to Althusser's state-centrism, grasp the "naturalization" of ascribed qualities as the subjective effect of a socially hegemonial way of speaking in which character traits are pinned to external features (skin color, gender) in the interest of preserving social and economic privileges and justifying the continued discrimination of certain groups.[25] It is obvious that both alternatives represent superior approaches to explaining the phenomena discussed above than the theories of recognition offered by Althusser and Butler. There may be an advantage to using the term "recognition" to characterize how the state ascribes typified qualities, as this draws our attention to the simultaneity of enticement and subordination, attraction and constriction, but this conceptual term hardly contributes to a more profound understanding of the processes involved. The proposals made by Ian Hacking or Sally Haslanger doubtlessly provide far more fruitful approaches.

The reason I have included Althusser's approach at all in my attempt to integrate my theoretical-historical findings was not to find indications of a convincing analysis of the conditions of male domination in marriage and the family. Instead my aim has been to show that Hegel's theory of recognition has a major gap, one which an entirely different idea of social recognition enables us to see. At this one point, i.e. the

---

[24] On such "looping effects", see Ian Hacking, The Social Construction of What? (Cambridge, MA: Harvard University Press, 1999).

[25] See Sally Haslanger, Resisting Reality: Social Construction and Social Critique (Oxford: Oxford University Press, 2012).

continued existence of domination in established relations of recognition, these two otherwise disparate traditions astonishingly overlap, whereby the second idea draws our attention to a weakness in the first, more fundamental idea of recognition. Not everything Hegel takes to be a relationship of mutual recognition is in fact free of domination, dependence and oppression. The social structure that encases or influences a relationship of recognition can cause certain individuals to be partially or entirely excluded from the freedoms granted to them in principle. In my summary of the European discourse on humans' dependence on others, we saw two such cases in which social structures hinder the realization of the normative potential of relations of recognition. In my discussion of a possible connection between Rousseau's notion of "amour propre" and Hegel's idea of mutual recognition, I mentioned that the German philosopher appeared to be familiar with psychological pathologies of the kind described by his predecessor on the other side of the Rhine in his Second Discourse. As we concluded on the basis of a number of passages in Hegel's *Philosophy of Right*, whenever individuals are deprived of access to relations of recognition to which they are legally entitled, they will tend to develop behaviors that are all but identical to the uninhibited practice of "amour propre" in the work of Rousseau. We could reasonably characterize this first instance of an obstruction of the potential of relations of recognition as "social closure" or "exclusion", as Max Weber terms it.[26] This signifies the common phenomenon, also

[26] Max Weber, Economy and Society (Berkeley: University of California Press, 2013).

described by Hegel, that individuals or entire groups, for whatever reason, are denied involvement in established relations of recognition, even though they fulfill all the necessary conditions for doing so. We might recall that Hegel mentions the emergence of the "rabble" as an instance of such exclusion, even if the psychological reaction to this injustice is neither pretension nor a craving for recognition. We encountered the second instance of a social-structural condition preventing relationships of recognition from unfolding their full normative potential in our examination of Althusser's distinctive idea of recognition based in French negativism. If we relate Althusser's idea back to Hegel's conceptual world, "ideological" constructions of the "natural" qualities of certain collectives are responsible for the fact that persons who recognize each other and are in principle recognized as being equal in fact possess unequal authority to define the nature of their relationship. In such a relation of recognition, the person to whom natural attributes are ascribed in a virtually ritual fashion – attributes which promise a greater amount of competence, public authority and other leadership qualities – will be able to use these apparent facts as an argument to preclude any further discussion and claim the sole normative authority to define social relations of recognition. The normative potential of mutual recognition in this second case is hollowed out by the shrinking of the space of potential reasons, making interpretations of shared norms seem natural. Therefore, it makes sense to call this an "argumentative" closure rather than a "social" closure of a relation of recognition.

This does not exhaust the social-structural conditions that can work to prevent subjects from making appropriate use of the normative authority granted to them in principle within an institutionalized relationship of mutual recognition. Both qualities ascribed to individual subjects as well as institutional rules can be experienced by those involved in such relations of recognition as unchangeable – this, too, is a case of "argumentative closure".[27] We must, however, take account of the fact that such obstructions cannot merely consist in some individuals having the authority to prevent other individuals from co-determining shared norms, for the reciprocal granting of a claim to co-determination is to be presupposed – otherwise, we would not be dealing with an institutionalized relation of recognition. The attempt to name a few examples of the constricting or undermining of this normative freedom was only meant to point out once again the surprising overlap between the conceptions circulating in European thought of the value and effect of interpersonal recognition. Even a concept of recognition such as that of Althusser, so alien to Hegel's conceptual world, remains connected to Hegel's social theory by revealing a grave weakness in it.

If we look at the contours we have given to Hegel's theory by comparing it to these other philosophical traditions, it can no longer be a surprise that there is another feature of his relations of recognition about whose constitutive significance Hegel left no doubt. It is not enough to conceive of such relationships of mutual recognition as being institutionalized,

---

[27] On the cultural construction of "inevitabilities", see Barrington Moore, *Injustice: The Social Bases of Obedience and Revolt* (London: Routledge, 1978), pp. 458–504.

since they are supposed to have come to prevail in social reality. In addition, their respective normative contents must consist of routine practices that have evolved into individual habits that have become second nature. Finally, their concrete shape in reality must be interpreted as being constantly controversial. Apart from Sartre, whose views on the eternal back-and-forth between subjects that objectify each other are absurd for reasons already mentioned above, Hegel is the only thinker in the European discourse on recognition who was convinced that our constitutive dependence on others gives rise to conflicts that can never ultimately be settled. Although Hegel did not always clearly emphasize this constitutive feature of relations of recognition (in his philosophy of right he even tends to downplay it, only allowing it to appear at the outermost margins of the text), on the whole it is clear that he had no doubt about its importance.[28] It is easy to see that the susceptibility of relationships of recognition to the most diverse forms of conflicts results from the fragility of the material making up these relationships. If the bonds of recognition consist merely in socially institutionalized norms among subjects who authorize each other to co-determine how these norms are interpreted and put into practice, then conflicts can constantly arise over the extent of their application as well as the circle of individuals to whom they apply. It should be noted, however, that this does

---

[28] On interpretations that go in this direction, see Honneth, *The Struggle for Recognition*; Georg W. Bertram and Robin Celikates, "Toward a Conflict Theory of Recognition", European Journal of Philosophy, 4 (2015), pp. 838–61.

not refer to those conflicts that can always result from differing interpretations of shared norms. Such disputes are a necessary part of any relation of recognition and make up the social form of existence of the norms underlying these relations; they cannot, therefore, be called conflicts in the true sense of the term. The latter kind of conflicts only emerge once we are no longer dealing with the interpretation of a norm in a clearly outlined and commonly accepted field of application, but with a case in which the objective borders of this field and the number of individuals within that field are a matter of debate. Returning to the example already mentioned above, it makes a big difference whether parents argue over responsibilities in the household in light of the norms of their partnership, or whether they argue about whether they should grant their children the right to have a say in such matters, thus including them in the parents' partnership. This example illustrates the difference between everyday disputes over the concrete application of a norm and conflicts over the thematic and personal extent of their area of application. This difference becomes much more significant, of course, when it comes to larger social disputes. It may be that Hegel, provided he did not just have the world spirit in mind, regarded such conflicts as the driving force behind the moral development of our relations of recognition over the course of human history.

With this vague outlook over a terrain of Hegel's theory of recognition that remains to be explored,[29] I have

---

[29] Even in light of more recent studies on Hegel's philosophy of history, I do not get the impression that we have a more clear conception of the social processes by which moral progress is, in Hegel's view, supposed to

reached the end of my attempt to bring some order into the array of conceptions of the meaning of social recognition since the beginning of modernity in a few European countries. At the very beginning of my synthesizing observations, I sought to justify why I employ Hegel's conception as a theoretical guide to how various ideas of recognition might be connected in spite of all of their methodological and substantive differences. Because I cannot exclude the possibility that there is still some skepticism about whether this decision has been based on implicit philosophical premises or – even worse – attachments to a certain culture of thought, once again I want to summarize the two reasons for my approach. My first idea was that Hegel's and Fichte's respective concepts of recognition do not name just any phenomenon in social life but its constitutive premise. Only by recognizing each other as persons who deserve the right to co-determine our shared norms do we fulfill the condition for a normatively regulated social existence. Although we do find indications of such an emphasis on the socially constitutive role of mutual recognition in the conception of an "inner spectator" in Scottish moral philosophy, they do not allow us to explain the origin and existence of socially regulative norms. If we concede that the Kantian-influenced tradition of German Idealism offers such a fundamental insight into the nature of social recognition, we still need a further argument

take place beneath the threshold of the world spirit, i.e. by virtue of the practices of historically situated subjects: Terry Pinkard, Does History Make Sense? Hegel on the Historical Shapes of Justice (Cambridge, MA: Harvard University Press, 2017); Joseph McCarney, Hegel on History (London: Routledge, 2000).

to make plausible why not both Hegel *and* Fichte, but merely the former should hold the key to an integral understanding of social recognition. Although both Hegel and Fichte recognized the socially constitutive role of recognition, only Hegel managed to free it from the transcendental realm and insert it into the social reality of a "spirit" that has become objective in the shape of institutional forms, moral habits and the living humans who deal with both. Because Hegel took this step beyond Fichte and thereby revealed his appreciation of the life-world existence of mutual recognition, I have chosen Hegel's theory as my guide to the other aspects emphasized by other traditional understandings of our dependence on others. That I have not taken appropriate account of all these different facets and have not been able to integrate all the features of recognition perceived in other traditions is partly the result of their great distance from Hegel's theory, and partly the result of the idiosyncratic observations from which they derive. Nevertheless, I feel the attempt to synthesize the various European traditions has significantly expanded our understanding of the constitutive role of recognition in social life. We now know that a theory of recognition inspired by Hegel must include a diagnosis of potential pathologies, an examination of constant potential obstructions, and, not to be forgotten, an analysis of the necessarily conflict-laden nature of mutual recognition.

Printed in the United States
by Baker & Taylor Publisher Services